HUMAN RESOURCE MANAGEMENT:
PEOPLE AND PERFORMANCE

Human Resource Management: People and Performance

Edited by
KEITH BRADLEY

Routledge
Taylor & Francis Group

LONDON AND NEW YORK

First published 1992 by Ashgate Publishing

Reissued 2018 by Routledge
2 Park Square, Milton Park, Abingdon, Oxon, OX14 4RN
52 Vanderbilt Avenue, New York, NY 10017

Routledge is an imprint of the Taylor & Francis Group, an informa business

Publisher's Note
The publisher has gone to great lengths to ensure the quality of this reprint but points out that some imperfections in the original copies may be apparent.

Disclaimer
The publisher has made every effort to trace copyright holders and welcomes correspondence from those they have been unable to contact.

A Library of Congress record exists under LC control number:

ISBN 13: 978-0-367-14594-1 (hbk)
ISBN 13: 978-0-429-05260-6 (ebk)

Contents

List of Tables

List of Figures

Foreword

Sir Terence Beckett KBE

This is a collection of papers which has its genesis in two highly successful conferences organised jointly by the LSE Business Performance Group and The Economist Conference Unit which both attracted some 200 European decision makers. The focus of attention, people and profits, is a theme which will become increasingly important in the 1990s as the demand for skills increases and their supply decreases and global competition intensifies. This book distinguishes itself by its interdisciplinary approach to these problems and its practical bent while not neglecting broader theoretical issues. It is therefore important reading for practising managers as well as students of management as we enter an entirely new and challenging era in employee relations.

The revolution which business went through in the 1980s replaced collectivism by enterprise. This meant that many of our management techniques and textbooks on human resource management and industrial relations became history. The timeliness of this collection of papers is that we have now reached the stage where it is important to review the bidding on personnel management and industrial relations experiments that occupied the 1980s and assess how relevant these really are to the future. Some past experiments have worked while others have not and some actually have been a drain on business performance.

The Business Performance Group, an innovative management research institute within the London School of Economics, raises some leading edge issues and makes some useful suggestions which managers and students alike should take into their arsenal as they prepare for the years ahead. The Group was founded in 1985 by Keith Bradley of the London School of Economics staff, with the broad goal of pursuing research relevant to managers in their efforts to improve the performance of business enterprises. In the past, most academics have deliberately kept their distance from commercial enterprises, lest their objectivity be threatened, and have made little effort to explain the relevance of their work to practising managers. A fundamental assumption of the Business Performance Group, in contrast, has been that academics need to develop closer, more collaborative relationships with the business community.

In the companies I have been associated with, I have always ensured that when we instituted change we also constructed an effective feedback loop. This frequently revealed a mismatch between our *espoused* and *actual* achievements. Without constructive feedback changes implemented by managers constitute a potential *loss* of business performance. Feedback can correct this and is therefore vitally important to management practice and sustained competitive advantage. This collection of papers which highlights some of the ongoing work associated with the Business Performance Group is important feedback on some current human resource issues in use today. By working in close partnership with the business community, the Business Performance Group focuses its efforts on issues of practical importance without sacrificing academic standards of quality. Business and academia have much to gain from working together. While their perspectives differ, business researchers and practitioners are both concerned with the same phenomena. When academics set the research agenda with an eye for managerial concerns their work is more likely to be relevant and useful. Moreover, close working relationships with business can give academics access to the kinds of data that are needed for outstanding research. Working with top management on issues of mutual concern is likely to be particularly productive in this regard. Far from necessitating a compromise in quality, joint ventures with business allow academics to undertake research of the scope and depth that would not otherwise be feasible. Over the past six years the Business Performance Group has become a leading international interdisciplinary research institute and has established a reputation as a centre of excellence in management research and education.

In the same spirit, members of the Group have established strong relationships with leaders of the business and policy communities, and have developed a distinctive interdisciplinary approach to understanding management issues. As Professor Michael Porter of the Harvard Business School has observed, the Business Performance Group's work helps to 'unscramble the way we measure and explain performance where the complexity of actual competition is recognized.' Michael Heseltine praised the Group for 'wielding a formidable axe in cutting away the props of a divided society' to reveal the value of co-operation among industry, government and academia.

Research undertaken by members of the Business Performance Group covers a wide spectrum. Recent publications by the Business

Performance Group include: *Managing Owners*, Cambridge University Press, *Business Performance in the Retail Sector*, Oxford University Press, *Enhancing Competition: The British Telecom-Mercury Duopoly*, Business Performance Group *Papers on Performance*, *Quality of Research in the City*, Business Performance Group *Papers on Performance*, and *Phone Wars*, Business Books.

Contributions to the *Human Resource Management* volume include practising managers from manufacturing, finance and services, policy makers, a leading business journalist, academics and researchers from six separate disciplines, (including information technology, sociology, industrial relations, accounting, economic history and economics). The volume is therefore truly interdisciplinary. From their different vantage points, all the contributors focus on the central question of how companies can best utilise people as a valuable asset to increase and sustain competitive advantage in the future.

Acknowledgements

Preparing this volume has been a concerted team effort. Invaluable help has been received from Joanne Bourne, Nancy Jackson, Brett Arends, Michael Lytle and the numerous contributors.

Further details about the London School of Economics Business Performance Group can be obtained from: Joanne Bourne, Business Performance Group, London School of Economics, Houghton Street, London WC2A 2AE. Telephone: 071 955 7744.

Biographies of Contributors

Professor Ian Angell. For the last six years Ian Angell has concentrated on strategic information systems and on organisational and national IT policies. He is at present acting as a consultant for a number of international organisations, and for one Eastern European and one Middle Eastern government. With a colleague, Dr Steve Smithson, he has recently published a book on this topic, *Information Systems Management: Opportunities and Risks*. Ian Angell obtained his first degree in Pure Mathematics from the University of Wales, and his doctorate, in Computer Applications to Algebraic Number Theory, from the University of London. All of his academic career has been spent at the University of London; he has held the Chair of Information Systems at the London School of Economics since 1986. Ian Angell is probably best known for his work in computer graphics, he has published ten books on the subject, the latest of which is *High Resolution Computer Graphics using C*.

Dr Keith Bradley. Keith Bradley is the Director of the LSE Business Performance Group. He has published widely on management, industrial policy, and employee relations. His books include *Worker Capitalism* (cited as 'one of the most outstanding books in the field of management, business, and labor relations'), *Cooperation at Work*, *Share Ownership for Employees*, *Managing Owners*, *Business Performance in the Retail Sector* and *Phone Wars*. He has contributed to *The Economist*, the *Financial Times*, the *Guardian*, and journals ranging from the *Harvard Business Review* to the *Review of Economic Studies*. A consultant to a variety of business, government, and international organizations, Dr Bradley has been a visiting professor at Harvard Business School and the University of Pennsylvania, a fellow of the Harvard Center for Business and Government, and a member of the Multinational Research Advisory Group of the Wharton School.

Dr Richard Caruso. Richard Caruso is President and Chief Executive Officer of LFC LifeSciences Corp. in the United States. An international authority on mentoring, Dr Caruso formerly practised as a Certified Public Accountant with Price Waterhouse & Co, and currently serves as a Director of the American Capital Mutual Funds and several other US corporations. He also serves on the international board of the LSE Business Performance Group.

Mr Greg Clark. Since joining the Business Performance Group two years ago as Project Director, Greg Clark has managed major consulting assignments with some of Britain's largest corporations. These include the effects of competition and regulation in the telecommunications industry and an examination of the compatibility of the organizational structure of a major UK multinational with its new strategy. He has written and lectured widely on pay and performance, including a keynote address to the CBI conference on Structuring Senior Executive Remuneration. Greg Clark was educated in Economics at Cambridge University and studied for his PhD at the London School of Economics.

Professor David Guest. David Guest is Head of the Department of Occupational Psychology at Birkbeck College, University of London. Prior to that he was a senior lecturer in Industrial Relations at the London School of Economics and also worked for a spell as Behavioural Science Adviser to British Rail. He is currently joint editor of the *British Journal of Industrial Relations* and is conducting research on commitment, culture change and human resource management effectiveness.

Professor Leslie Hannah. Leslie Hannah is the author of *The Rise of the Corporate Economy* and other books on modern business. He has taught at the Universities of Oxford, Essex, Cambridge, Hitotsubashi and Harvard and is currently at the London School of Economics. Leslie Hannah also serves on the LSE Business Performance Group steering committee.

Professor Stephen Hill. Stephen Hill is Professor of Sociology at the London School of Economics. He is an expert on Total Quality Management, the management of technological innovation in manufacturing, the directors of British companies and the restructuring of the business enterprise in Eastern Europe. He has published widely in the sociology of work and employment and has contributed also to the analysis of ideology. His books include: *The Dockers* and *Competition and Control at Work*; and as co-author, *The Dominant Ideology Thesis*, *The Penguin Dictionary of Sociology*, *Sovereign Individuals of Capitalism* and *Dominant Ideologies*.

Mr Christopher Huhne. Christopher Huhne is Business Editor of *The Independent* and *The Independent on Sunday*, editing the business sections and writing a weekly economics column and commentaries.

Prior to this he was Economics Editor for the *Guardian*. Christopher Huhne has published widely. His recent publications include: *The ECU report: the single European currency* and *Real World Economics: essays on imperfect markets and fallible governments*.

Dr Paul Johnson. Paul Johnson is an expert on the social and economic consequences of demographic change and population ageing in Europe and an associate member of the Business Performance Group. He has published and broadcast widely on pensions and employment issues and is a lecturer in Social History at the London School of Economics.

Sir Leonard Peach. Leonard Peach is currently Director of Personnel and Corporate Affairs for IBM UK Ltd and, at one time was Group Director of Personnel for IBM Europe, Africa and the Middle East based in Paris. He was seconded from IBM to the National Health Service between 1985-89 initially as Director of Personnel and later as the Chief Executive of the NHS Management Board. He was President of the Institute of Personnel Management between 1983-85. He is currently President of the Manpower Society and of the Association of Management and Business Education; Chairman of Skillbase Ltd and of the Policy Studies Institute; Vice Chairman of the Polytechnic of Central London; a Non-executive Director of the Nationwide Anglia Building Society and of the Royal London Hospital. Sir Leonard Peach also serves on the LSE Business Performance Group international board.

Dr Riccardo Peccei. Riccardo Peccei is lecturer in Industrial Relations at the London School of Economics. Prior to that he worked at the Tavistock Institute and at Imperial College. He has worked on the Industrial Democracy in Europe project and on the evaluation of change and analysis of organizational effectiveness of public sector organizations and national training initiatives. Recent research has focused on evaluation of management development, on the changing role of middle management and on organizational commitment.

Mr John Redwood MP. John Redwood was promoted to Minister of State at the Department of Trade and Industry in November 1990. Prior to this he held the position of Parliamentary Under Secretary of State at the same Department. John Redwood entered Parliament in 1987. From 1973-77 he worked in the City as an investment adviser and corporate finance director. He was adviser to the Treasury and Civil Service Select Committee in 1981 and was Head of the Prime Minister's policy unit from 1983-85. From 1985-89 he was non-executive director of Norcros plc and chairman from 1987-89. John Redwood was formerly a member of the LSE Business Performance Group international board.

Mrs Steve Shirley OBE. Steve Shirley is the Founder Director of the FI Group plc, a recognised leader in innovative work methodologies. Mrs Shirley's action oriented management style and emphasis on ethics and professional standards led to an OBE for services to industry in 1980 and the Freedom of the City of London in 1987. A pioneer of participative management, she achieved another of her aims when FI moved into effective control of its workforce in 1991. She currently serves on the Council of the Industrial Society which promotes the active involvement of people in their work and on Lord Young's National Council for Vocational Qualifications. She is President of the British Computer Society.

Ms Patrice Rosenthal. Patrice Rosenthal is a researcher at the London School of Economics. She completed an MSc at the School in Industrial Relations and Personnel Management. Her research interests include managerial career development, women and work, and attribution theory.

Dr Simon Taylor. Simon Taylor is a Fellow of St Catharine's College, Cambridge, sometime consultant to the World Bank, and former project director with the Business Performance Group. During his tenure in the Group he was responsible for managing major research projects and contributing to Business Performance Group lectures and seminars and representing the Group in a number of press and current affairs programmes. He is currently working as an analyst in the City. After gaining a first class honours degree in economics at Cambridge and winning the Wrenbury Scholarship, he undertook graduate research work at Oxford University and the London School of Economics where he gained his PhD. For two years he was an Overseas Development Institute Fellow at the Central Bank of Lesotho. His publications include *Business Performance in the Retail Sector*, *Research Quality in the City* and *Enhancing Competition: The British Telecom-Mercury Duopoly* (from the Business Performance Group *Papers on Performance* series).

Dr Eamonn Walsh. Eamonn Walsh is a specialist in accounting and finance. Sometime Visiting Professor at the University of California (Berkeley). Currently a Visiting Professor at New York University. His work focuses on international financial management. Editor of *European Accounting News*.

INTRODUCTION

1

People and Performance

John Redwood

The theme *People and Performance* is a vital one for the 1990s. British business has been through many downs and some ups in the last two decades. The 1970s were years of pressure: of crisis, of little profitability, little luck and little enterprise. The times were against business. Profits were squeezed by high taxation and by difficult trading circumstances. This was a period of aggressive trade union activity, in which management found itself fighting a series of rearguard actions.

The end of the decade brought a new maturity, as managers began to fight back. As companies struggled to weather the 1979-81 recession, the emphasis fell heavily on the balance sheet; on the roles of the finance director and the accountant. The press and other commentators stressed the need to tackle what was perceived as *the union problem*. The period was marked by a few rather long and bitter strikes, culminating with the miners' dispute in the mid 1980s. Looking back, however, we can see the turning of the tide. Strikes gradually came under control, and the trade union problem seemed less fierce by the end of the decade.

The later 1980s brought a period of relative corporate success and prosperity. Profits rose dramatically. Real returns on capital became highly acceptable for the average industrialist, not just the exceptionally successful ones. This was a period of large scale acquisitions, as companies decided they could grow best by acquiring their neighbour, their competitor or even a company in a completely different business. It seemed that two plus two would always equal five – though in retrospect some people have questioned whether these acquisitions were deeds of corporate heroism or folly.

The 1990s will be rather different from any of these three eras, which were marked by rather one-sided and limited perceptions of industrial and management life. The future will be characterised by a combination of extremely competitive conditions and considerable prosperity and reasonable growth in most marketplaces. Higher income consumers will be increasingly sophisticated: they may be *green*, they may be finicky about the level of quality and service provided. The 1990s will be an interesting marketplace in which to compete, and if companies apply appropriate management strategies, they will do extremely well. If managers do not pay attention to products, quality, innovation, changing customer demands and preferences, then life will be much more difficult.

Surviving in this very competitive world will mean managing change sensibly and prudently. Management strategies will have to change enough to keep pace with evolving customer needs, but not so much as to be in permanent revolution and chaos. The premium will be on business skills and on people; it will indeed be a case of *people meaning profits*.

By way of introduction to this volume, I would like to draw attention to four subjects that I think will be important on the industrial and business agenda in the 1990s. These are quality, design, customer service and the mass customization of manufacturing.

Quality

In my previous incarnation as chairman of an industrial company, I was very pleased to have a management team who believed strongly in the idea of quality. I realised this when I first travelled round the group and saw the very different experience of the various operating subsidiaries. The group set itself the task of getting every company up to BS 5750 or the equivalent within eighteen months.

It was a fascinating exercise. Some units were able to say, 'But we did that five years ago. We wouldn't sell anything unless we were up to that standard. What we're interested in now is total quality – involving the workforce in the quality concept'. At the other end of the spectrum some people would say, 'Oh, we don't need all those inspectors and bits of paper that quality standards entail. It's just an added cost, and what we need is to keep our costs under control'.

The challenge to any executive team is to find a way of showing any doubter that quality standards – the first phase of a total quality effort – are not an optional extra you could bolt on if you had a bit of spare money. In fact, quality does not necessarily add cost if you do it correctly. Quality has to be a spirit that brings enthusiasm to the whole group. A properly conducted quality effort can bring all kinds of benefits in the way these companies were running their businesses. This is a feat of leadership that has to be performed by each chief executive or key decision-maker in each subsidiary. It is a good test of how good people are: can they see something positive in quality? How can they identify it? How can they lead their team of people into believing in it and making it work for them?

It is quite easy to establish the first selling point: adhering to quality assurance standards will encourage more people to buy your products. This is especially the case among large and powerful government or corporate customers. Indeed, with these customers you may not be able to sell your product at all unless it meets the required standard, because the purchasing agents will be concerned about protecting their own position. Purchasing agents tend to be clerks, not entrepreneurs, and they want to be able to justify their decision to their boss if something goes wrong. As a result, companies will evolve procedures, vetting and competitive tenders based on quality standards. So the first and the easy part of selling the idea of quality to any company is explaining that quality is a salesman's joy.

The next phase of a quality programme – total quality – becomes more complicated as it starts to affect the way people carry out their jobs. Nobody likes to feel that he or she is being criticised from the outside. Telling employees that they are incompetent and must improve is likely to create tension within the business and drive things from bad to worse. But there are constructive ways, that can be found, of explaining to people the importance of quality. For example, you can point out that controlling quality as part A moves down the production line and is bolted on to part B will produce savings. This is often the case even when the job must be performed more accurately and perhaps more slowly and additional inspections are required. Under such conditions the reject rate may fall off dramatically. Furthermore, savings might come in warranty costs, or in the significant reduction of customer dissatisfaction. Cutting the failure rate from 5 to 0.5 per cent could represent a huge saving in management time that might otherwise be spent sifting customer complaints, warding off legal actions, paying out monies to those who had been wronged and so forth.

The best way to introduce quality is to explain to people that there was something in it for them and for their company. Better quality can reduce inventory levels, cut reject rates and increase customer satisfaction. It can mean profits. But because success depends on popular support in the factory, managers have to convince employees that quality makes their jobs more interesting and the company's products more worthwhile. (For a further discussion of quality, see chapter 9.)

Design

The second factor which will be vital to business success in the 1990s is design. In the sixties and seventies – to overstate the point a little, by looking at the average rather than the outstanding – British industry was driven largely by engineering concepts and by an attitude that might be summed up as 'this is what we make, and so somebody ought to buy it'. The nationalised steel company might invest in capacity to supply say 40 million tons without really asking itself who would buy the product, to what standard it should be made, or what alloys and what mixtures should be used. When it turned out that they could sell only 15 million tons, that made a significant difference to the arithmetic of the project. Similarly, under the Ryder plan British Leyland was supposed to satisfy 40 per cent of all demand for automobiles. By the time the plan was fully implemented, however, less than 20 per cent of cars sold in the United Kingdom were made by British Leyland.

In this instance the failure was primarily one of design. People looked at the cars the British firms were making and decided that they would really rather have a Volkswagen, Renault or Fiat. As a result, all the efforts of the British industry – to sort out labour relations, to mount a major investment programme paid for by the taxpayer – did not accomplish much, because the design was wrong. Given the choice that comes with a relatively free market, the British public said: 'yes, we do want the British industry to flourish, we do want it to be supported, but that's not my job. I'm going to buy a Volkswagen'. And so they did.

To survive in the competitive conditions of the 1990s, companies will have to ensure that their designers have clout in internal discussions. At the same time, the designer will have to be someone who can maintain good relationships with the marketing director and with the production director, who after all has to be able to make the product at a sensible price in a reasonable way. Design must be informed by an understanding of the marketplace. Above all, design must be functional, aesthetically pleasing, and popular with those who are going to buy the product.

Designers must be given headroom. It will become more important to look around for design ideas from the past, from competitors, and from shop floor employees. You might be surprised at how many people have got a design idea they have hesitated to express because they have always been squashed before. Do not cast these ideas aside because they come from the *wrong* place: encourage and test them. Only then can managers enjoy the luxury of choosing from a number of different projects that people want to launch. This is significantly better than trying to squeeze one new idea from a group of recalcitrant and terrified employees who have been told that bright ideas can be costly or risky.

Customer service

The third area, and perhaps the core issue for the 1990s, is customer service. This is becoming a critical concern for industrial as well as the service companies. In the United Kingdom the debate has focused on the wrong issue. It has either concentrated on whether we are giving adequate support to manufacturing industry, which we are told is the only source of wealth, or whether we are becoming a sort of *Disneyland economy*, in which we all hold service sector jobs that do not really count and do not generate any wealth at all.

Statistics showing that the service sector has grown at the expense of manufacturing may be misleading. For example, under the conventions of the national accounts, when ICI undertakes its own computing, that activity is subsumed in the manufacturing total. But if ICI managers contract out their departments' computing to a service bureau, the statistics will show a decline in manufacturing activity and an increase in service sector activity. In reality, nothing much has changed – except that ICI has now presumably got a better deal for its computing. But such a shift contributes to the impression that manufacturing is declining and the service sector is swallowing up the wealth creating part of the economy.

The distinction between manufacturing and service sectors can therefore be a false dichotomy. Service has always mattered; it was never the case that you could create wealth only by manufacturing things. What is the use of manufacturing motor cars if there are no filling stations or garages to service cars? In today's marketplace, the fusion of product and service has become more important than ever. The success of the British economy will depend, to a great extent, upon the mutual deployment of manufacturing skills and customer service.

Proximity to customers is crucial since they are often the best source of information. For example, I once visited the showroom of a company that made kitchen units. The broad range on display had a family resemblance. When I asked the woman in charge of the showroom which units she herself preferred, she at first gave the officially approved reply that she liked all of them. Her manager beamed. When I persisted and asked which ones she had bought for her own home, she looked very sheepish and said she would rather not answer that question. Now her manager looked extremely worried, but I pressed for an answer. 'This lady is a potential customer', I said. 'She is not at the moment buying this product, but let's find out what she really wants.' Eventually the potential customer admitted that she wanted something slightly different. Instead of melamine wall units, she wanted something more free-standing, something that looked like a Welsh dresser. She did not want to buy actual antiques – she would rather the units held together properly, did not wobble and were clean – but she wanted something that looked like an antique. In effect, she had put her finger on a design and market research point of critical importance to the company: the kitchen market was moving towards a different concept. Shortly after my conversation, the company launched a look-alike, free-standing Welsh dresser unit which sold very well. It is never a bad idea to consult the showroom staff.

Mass customization

The final point on my agenda for the 1990s is flexible manufacturing itself, which follows naturally from the customer driven competitive marketplace. We are moving towards the sort of *mass customization* that the Japanese have already attained. Flexible manufacturing units will have to be able to switch batches rapidly, change runs, and respond to individual customer orders – while still enjoying economies of scale.

Successful businesses in the 1990s will be those that can respond almost immediately to a demand for product variation – producing something that is rather like the things it makes normally but responding to some slight difference in customer preference. Perhaps the product is embellished with a special logo or made to slightly different measurements. To respond to such demands, manufacturers need to have the software already installed, so that employees can simply type in the additional requirements and be ready to dispatch the product in a few days.

I am told that a Japanese car buyer can place an order on Monday morning, choosing among dozens of variations in styling and features (cloth trim, types of stereo, and so on), and the car will be manufactured and delivered to the customer's home within five days. That is quite a humbling thought, given the stock-piles and the slow response times that still characterise some sectors of British industry.

To match the Japanese capability for mass customization, British industry must build flexibility into its operations. That will mean investing in technology and people: individuals driven by the urge to understand customers and look after their needs by supplying the appropriate products. British manufacturers will need people who are properly motivated, not afraid of new ideas and change, and who can learn from their experiences and traditions of success within their own businesses.

There will be difficulties in obtaining people with the necessary skills, (see chapters 12 and 15). Managers will need to be imaginative about recruiting, training and using their employees wisely. For example, there are still many married women in Britain who would like some kind of paid employment but are unable to work full-time. They may occasionally have to take a day off when a child is sick; they may have to leave work to go home and sort out a crisis. Mothers usually work extremely hard, and they have a discipline and a sense of responsibility and purpose that comes from running a family. Many businesses will find it pays to organise a creche for their employees. Working mothers will be able to pay the relatively modest charges that will enable the creche to operate at breakeven, and the company will be able to tap into a large pool of potential employees (about a quarter of the population) who currently think they are debarred from working even though they have much-needed skills and attitudes. (For a discussion of how one employer has tapped this resource, see chapter 6.)

Meanwhile, industry is also discovering that it is possible to home-grow many of the skills it needs, by helping with technical and training programmes, and perhaps recreating, in a modern idiom, something of the old apprentice scheme, in which managers recruit people, pay them reasonably, train them and promote them as their aptitudes develop.

Blending small and large

British companies need to adopt an organizational form which blends the strengths of the small and the big company. The small company is likely to be entrepreneurial, headed by a key leader who has a brilliant idea and the driving force to carry the business through its early years. Small companies may have harmonious relationships with their employees, because they all know each other personally and all want to succeed. Small companies may be more likely to adopt a sensible plan for employee profit participation or even share participation.

The problem for the small business is that it might not be big enough to have all the skills that it requires. It may be skilled at production and bad at finance, or skilled at selling and bad at production. It is very easy for skills to be out of balance in a small company, because at critical stages of development it may simply not be possible for the company to take on an additional full-time person with the necessary experience and skills. Conversely, the big company is seldom short of the overhead of management. It will have the personnel, finance and production specialists, although these may differ in ability, rank and weight within the company, causing political tensions. There will be a professionalism among the management of large corporations.

The danger for the big company is that it will become ossified or bureaucratic. The lines of communication are too long; there is too much paper and too little business; too much talking to colleagues and not enough talking to customers; too much attention to internal politics and not enough to the wider public, to the shareholders and to those who buy the goods and services. In a large company under autocratic control, where the people at the top manage by fear rather than by leadership, the wellsprings of entrepreneurship can dry up.

The successful enterprise of the 1990s will blend the best of both small and large organizations. Larger companies will need to find ways to accelerate promotion for talented and hardworking people, and to encourage entrepreneurship from within, at every level. In some respects the larger company may find it relatively easy to give people scope for career development. A young entrepreneur with discretion over £3 million in a small company could bankrupt it by making a mistake. At Shell or BP, a bad outcome with a venture of that size would be far less damaging. In all companies, however, it is important to manage mistakes and keep them under control. But it would be wrong to try to prevent mistakes altogether, since people learn from them.

Smaller companies may need to move toward greater use of part-time consultancy and advice. The guidance of an experienced, senior non-executive advisor can be particularly valuable to a small company in its formative stages – in suggesting how to raise money in the City, for example, or how to handle a particular new kind of customer or contract. There may be opportunities for entrepreneurial professional services businesses, which would rent out finance directors or skilled lawyers by the day rather than by the year. The partnership style, which already works in accounting and legal professions, might be taken into areas such as marketing and production. A small company might need first rate production engineer for three months, or for one day a week, but could neither afford nor need to hire such a person full-time.

Small and large businesses have much to learn from each other, and we may see more interchange and joint ventures. Managers in large corporations sometimes spin off small businesses of their own and work under contract for their former boss. Big businesses should think about accommodating that phenomenon, rather than regarding it as a kind of failure. Small business owners may decide in the end they want to merge or enter a joint venture with a bigger business, or they may collaborate with the bigger businesses who are their customers.

Business-academic links in the future

Running a business and managing change in the 1990s will be a complicated and difficult task. As we wrestle with this challenge, links between the business and academic worlds will be increasingly impor-tant in order to encourage the useful exchange of ideas and practices. One prominent theme is likely to be the need to encourage full-scale employee participation. In successful companies, practically every employee will be in some way involved in serving the customer, in generating ideas which are required to sustain competitive advantage. The 1990s will be a testing time for business. The companies which successfully focus on the issues we have mentioned, particularly people issues, and engage in greater openness to ideas and new ventures will be profitable.

2

The Human Capital Audit and Business Performance

Keith Bradley

Introduction

The idea that people are crucial to the effective running of a commercial organization is nothing new. Even in the early 1800s, far sighted employers had identified the gains to be reaped by taking their employees seriously. As organizations grew larger, becoming multidivisional and bureaucratic, the need to keep track of an increasing number of employees gave rise to the personnel function around the turn of the present century. Information, payments and rewards were typically organised through a separate department of the company.

In the 1970s and early 1980s, the growing competitive threat to United States and United Kingdom firms stimulated a search, first for productivity and then for innovation and flexibility. The Japanese example indicated the importance of not only investing in fixed capital, but making full use of the skills and commitment of the workforce. This notion became codified in the idea of human resource management.

Looking at employees as *human resources* focused attention on the potential for more efficient use of that pool of talent and ability, and for longer term innovation – potential that earlier management methods and styles had neglected. The creation of a separate, specialised personnel function had diverted general managers' attention from a responsibility that was properly their own: exploring and enhancing employees' contributions to long term profit potential. The recognition of this gap was of considerable practical importance.

Yet, a decade after human resource management began to percolate into mainstream management consciousness, much remains to be done to integrate the organization's human capital with its physical and financial capital. Too often, the only real change has been to change a label from *personnel* to *human resources*. Just as a video from the chairman exhorting a new commitment to zero defects may be all that comes of a *major initiative on quality*, so the new human resource management has failed to realise its potential.

The danger is that human resource management will come to be seen as just another fad, a bright idea that promised enduring gains in productivity and yet somehow came to very little. Human factors, job enrichment, quality: all flavours of the month for a while, each leaving a residue of changed practice, but never quite fulfilling their apparent promise. This would be a potentially disastrous outcome: the social side of the business is likely to become more important in the 1990s, rather than less. Demographic pressures will make staffing increasingly difficult even as intense international competition heightens the need for organizational flexibility and adaptability. Managing change is the issue of the day, and this task is quintessentially about people.

Why has human resource management got into a rut? A large part of the explanation lies in the failure to integrate conventional models of business performance with the complex and subtle – but crucial – dimension of human capital. Using a case study, we illustrate new methods of synthesis and measurement pioneered in research programmes carried out by the LSE Business Performance Group which achieve this integration, give insight into the role of the human side of business, and generate operationally useful management data.

Problems of integration

Two central problems stand in the way of a more effective and consistent approach to human capital issues in business. The first is the lack of integration between the analytical tools used to study the firm's external competitive environment and its optimal financial and production strategies, and the analysis and management of the human capital of the enterprise. Over the last few decades, management has made good use of a structured and directed methodology for examining a range of central business questions: Is the firm correctly positioned relative to the product market? Is its financial structure optimal? Is the business portfolio properly balanced? Is the internal configuration of productive equipment the most efficient feasible for the output demands? These methods pay scant attention to the human side of the business, however.

Although some aspects of the firm's *black box* have been opened up, notably on the technology and production side, there remains a large *black hole* that absorbs all the awkward issues: change, organizational culture, career development, recruitment and training. These typically boil down to considerations of people.

In many firms, major management decisions are heavily influenced by strategy consultants whose ideas were developed a quarter century ago by applying traditional principles of industrial economics to business organizations. As a consequence contemporary management decisions make superficial reference to, or even omit entirely, a major dimension of their company's operations: its human side. The human resource management approach at least places this dimension on the chief executive's agenda, but identifies it as a distinct set of tasks and strategies to be formulated by a specialised group of managers. This schism is potentially very damaging. The strategy that seems best from the production or finance point of view, may be severely flawed, or even inoperable from a social capital perspective.

If human resource management has never been successfully integrated with other aspects of management, that is partly because there has been no consistent methodology for defining, analyzing and measuring the human capital of business enterprises. Many books purport to explain how to measure the effectiveness of human resources in the business. Unfortunately, the approaches they suggest make major information demands on companies without getting close to the meaningful data. Often sweeping assumptions are implicitly made about mechanistic links between, for example, training and subsequent productivity. The approach is naive and unrigorous, and confines itself to a very narrow class of information.

Progress in thinking about the human side of business will require an operationally useful framework within which a broader range of data on the human capital of the business can be collected and analyzed; ideally information will be gathered in a consistent manner that can be replicated across firms as well as within an individual organization. Moreover this effort should not be confined to the personnel ghetto; rather the framework should be fully articulated with the financial and physical sides of the business in a unified whole. For a number of years now this has been on the agenda of the LSE Business Performance Group and rewards of this approach are beginning to filter through into management publications. (See Bradley and Nejad, 1989; Taylor, 1989; Caruso, 1990, for a fuller discussion of these important methodological issues.)

Of course there can never be a perfect decision-making process which integrates all possible data to deliver a *how to run your business* instruction. But a coherent and comprehensive framework for collecting and analyzing management information is feasible. The experience of Showcase International (a pseudonym) illustrates the Business Performance Group approach and demonstrates how a division of a major international manufacturing firm used an analysis of its human capital as a vital component of its new competitive strategy.

Showcase International: a case study

Showcase International is a multinational company producing high valued added manufactured goods predominantly for the Western Europe and North American markets. The firm has been cited in the United Kingdom financial press as epitomising the renaissance of British manufacturing in the 1980s. Judged by such financial criteria as return on capital, return on fixed assets, and real turnover growth, Showcase appeared to be doing very well in 1988, when the Business Performance Group examined its United Kingdom division, which concentrates on the upper quality end of the company's product range. Moreover, the company had stressed its commitment to investment in research and development, which was an important part of its competitive advantage, in terms of both process and product innovation.

The study began as an exploration of the overall position of the company in relation to its competitors. The directors were clearly confident that they would emerge as successful in both relative and absolute terms, although this impression was not based on any definite information. A sense of how well other firms were doing gets around an industry, and Showcase was pleased with itself.

The first stage of our analysis investigated the longer term context of the firm's recent success. Emerging from the depth of the manufacturing recession in 1981-82, the company's performance was indeed encouraging, registering a strong upward trend in output, turnover and profitability. However, a look at the twenty five year record revealed a less impressive picture. The firm had barely recovered to the output peak it had reached in the 1970s, and most of the 1980s recovery was a scramble to regain its long term trend. Profitability had improved somewhat, but, as figure 2.1 shows, in absolute terms, the company's performance was not nearly as good as it had been for the decade up to the mid-1970s.

Going beyond the purely financial data, the next stage of analysis examined economic productivity. The picture here was encouraging, with a very strong increase in output per employee, pushing productivity to new heights. Comparable productivity had not been achieved since the 1960s, when the average rate of growth was lower. This appeared to be very good news: strong fundamental productivity growth should permit financial success so long as the product design and marketing are correctly handled (see chapter 1). Showcase's rising turnover suggested it was on the right track.

Figure 2.1 Showcase International: Pre-tax real profit

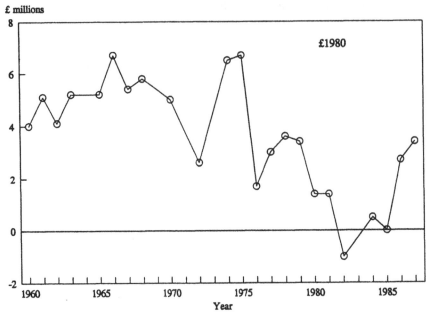

A comparison with the earlier period of high productivity growth revealed a striking difference, however. Whereas the rise in labour productivity during the 1960s had been supported by a major capital investment programme, fixed capital had not changed significantly since the early 1970s (see figure 2.2). In other words, the productivity rise in the 1980s had been achieved with the existing installed plant. This observation suggested that Showcase owed its success to a radical improvement in the manner of organising work, precisely the issue that the United Kingdom (and to a degree the United States) had apparently neglected for so long. Investment is futile unless it is used effectively. While avoiding heavy investments, Showcase had apparently squeezed dramatically higher output from the same physical resources. Consequently, the balance sheet was strong and cash flow was highly satisfactory.

Doubts about Showcase's performance began to crystallise after a comparison with close competitors, a small number of companies that also sold to the upper quality segment of the market. The comparisons revealed that Showcase's financial success was not unusual. On the contrary, strong demand growth had led to higher turnover across the industry. In addition, estimates of the productivity of competitor firms suggested that Showcase's strong rate of productivity growth was actually less than the industry average. Competitors were doing

Figure 2.2 Showcase International: Fixed assets per employee

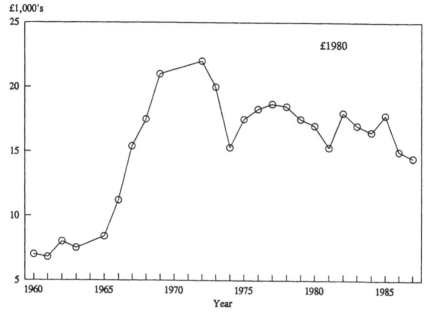

markedly better towards the end of the period. Showcase's competitors, it turned out, had all undertaken major investment programmes. Their productivity could be directly associated with a major new commitment to fixed assets. Showcase on the other hand had squeezed its new output without such a commitment (see figure 2.3).

On the surface, it might appear that Showcase was to be congratulated for generating much higher profits, at least for a few years, while taking on less debt than its competitors. There was some doubt on the part of the Business Performance Group, however, whether the profit improvement could be sustained, given the investments made by competitors.

This is the point at which reliance on economic data and the typical management strategy framework, based on industrial economics, begins to run out of steam. To settle the issue with any satisfaction requires a more detailed exploration of the internal characteristics of the firm, emphasising the work process. The Business Performance Group's work therefore moved to examine two sorts of internal data: *hard* (relatively easy to quantify) and *soft* (somewhat more subjective in nature). Despite the misgivings of economists and accountants, *soft* data can be crucially useful in understanding enterprise performance (see Bradley and Taylor, 1992).

**Figure 2.3 Showcase International and its major competitors:
Fixed assets per employee**

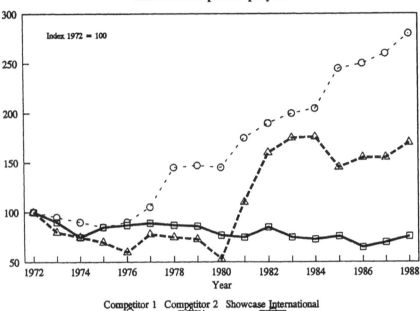

Competitor 1   Competitor 2   Showcase International

Analysis of the work process began with the structure of the firm's
human capital: the distribution of staff in terms of age, occupation, level
in the hierarchy, time with the company and other characteristics. Our
study also investigated such issues as the family size and financial
position of the staff (eg, savings and investments). Some of this data
could be supplied directly by the company; the rest was collected by a
detailed confidential questionnaire survey of the workforce.[1]

Developed after an intensive process of cooperation between the
researchers and the company officers, the survey instrument was
designed to meet the twin requirements of relevance and reliability. The
relevance criterion was tested by extensive piloting, and a considerable
amount of feedback from staff at all levels of the company. Reliability
was built in through careful use of consistency checks and very large
samples, ensuring that even small subsets of a department would
contain a statistically useable number. Besides gathering information
on the personal characteristics of the workforce, the survey included
some two hundred attitudinal questions on a wide range of issues, from
safety to the organization of the work, technology, training, communication and managerial style.

The preliminary analysis indicated a striking pattern: over the last
twenty years, the ratio of managers and administrators to rank and file

employees had increased substantially within Showcase. In relation to the number of semi-skilled and unskilled workers, the number of managers had risen by around one half. The proportion of administrators had also risen substantially (see figure 2.4). The establishment of a research laboratory within the firm accounted for only part of this change. More detailed analysis of the questionnaire data revealed that a wave of promotions to supervisory positions had occurred in the early 1980s.

Figure 2.4 Showcase International: Composition of labour force over time

1968   1978   1988

Managers/Supervisors   Administrators   Workers

The results of the opinion audit were highly instructive. The overall audit of the company's management-employee relations was far from favourable. Employees voiced considerable discontent on the issues of communication and perceived management competence. Moreover, there were strong indications of dissatisfaction with the role of the supervisors in the main plant. Supervisors were widely perceived to be interfering and less than competent (see figure 2.5). The dissatisfaction scores at Showcase were considerably higher than for comparable firms previously studied by our research team, suggesting a significant problem.

Going further, the researchers contrasted the perceptions of supervisors and supervisees on a range of matters. Perhaps the most remarkable findings had to do with training, an issue on which the two groups' perceptions diverged sharply. Workers felt that the supervisors did not give them enough support as they learned new tasks, and generally made it more difficult to do the job right. Supervisors, on the other hand, were confident that they were doing quite enough to ensure that supervisees had access to all the relevant data needed to do the job properly.

Cross referencing these results with a wide range of other indicative attitude questions confirmed the picture of a very unhappy set of

Figure 2.5 Showcase International: Dissatisfaction with supervisors

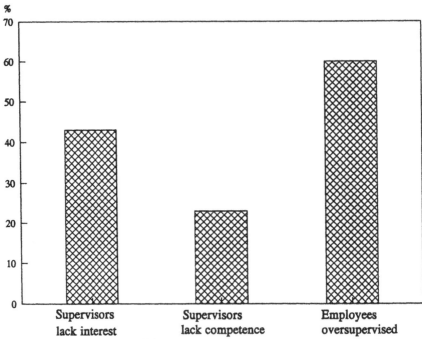

employees, especially in those sections of the work process where the speed-up had most increased the demands on workers. The evidence suggested that Showcase was using excessive supervision, whether through deliberate policy or by misconception, to squeeze added labour productivity. But the evidence also suggested that this state of affairs was not sustainable. Labour turnover had been increasing in the company, despite relatively high levels of unemployment in the general economy. The turnover was alarmingly high among some of the younger, semi-skilled workers that the company needed to keep its productivity surge intact.

In short, the long term sustainability of Showcase's productivity boom was questionable, and so therefore was its profit surge. The management commitment to research and development might have been a way out, if it had led to the implementation of labour-saving techniques that could relieve workers' dissatisfaction. Upon investigation, however, this stated commitment turned out to be much weaker than it appeared. Total research and development spending was a very low proportion of turnover and profits. Comparative data for the direct competitors was of course not available, but comparisons with firms in other sectors suggested that Showcase was not doing nearly enough to sustain its long term product quality commitment, let alone innovate in its manufacturing process to relieve pressure in the workplace.

In fact the situation was even worse. A significant fraction of Showcase's spending on research and development had gone into training key laboratory staff. The rate of labour turnover amongst this group was particularly high and was associated with very high levels of dissatisfaction with the organization of the work. This represented a significant *hidden* cost which the research technique was able to quantify and bring to the management's attention (see chapter 12). The loss of these employees was especially worrying because the laboratory played a critical role in the company's competitive strategy.

In principle, training for workers might have relieved some of Showcase's problems, and indeed the firm had made some efforts along these lines. Questionnaire data showed, however, that the impact of training on the company was disappointing. Many workers felt the training offered was of little use, regarding it as a perk with little intrinsic interest. At the same time, there appeared to be a tremendous demand for training of the right kind, training that would actually improve workers' ability to do the job. Very few employees reported that managers had ever talked with them about what training was actually useful or desirable. All in all, the analysis suggested a possibly unsustainable productivity growth rate and poorly used training resources.

Confronted with this discouraging picture, some of the company officers became defensive about their failure to invest in more equipment at the outset, as their competitors had. The workforce had been resistant to change, they asserted. Yet the Business Performance Group employee audit showed that a very large number of workers saw new equipment and technology as important to long term success. There was strong support for such investment, even if it might lead to job losses. The management were quite incorrect in their assumption that any attempt to introduce new investment would lead to conflicts and disruption.

The major achievements of the Showcase study were:

1) It demonstrated the respects in which Showcase was performing successfully, relative to its own history and its main competitors. Productivity was good, but not remarkable for the industry. Turnover growth was not significantly better than in the past and merely followed the industry norm. Profitability was strong, largely reflecting the fact that the productivity gains were achieved without large scale capital expenditure.

2) A range of other information was used to investigate the sustainability of the current strategy. Findings suggested strong

grounds for concern. The strategy appeared to be closely related to excessive supervision and poor perception of management by the workforce.

3) Our study investigated certain management beliefs about the company and its workforce, beliefs that had a direct influence on strategic thinking. Some of these perceptions were shown to be seriously misinformed, and very different production and financial strategies were revealed as feasible and desirable.

4) A powerful database was provided that could be used in the design and implementation of new strategies, whose impact could be tested and quantified by a systematic replication of the study at a later date. Quantitative indicators were provided that would supply *benchmarks* for future performance.

In sum, the study provided a powerful audit of the company's performance, going well beyond the usual competitive analysis to get at some of the finer details of the organization of the work process. The results jolted some of management's cherished beliefs, but also provided an invaluable tool for designing management strategy for the future, based far more securely on reliable data and interpretation.

Human resource management in the 1990s

In the chapters that follow, business leaders and academics examine specific areas in which human resource management will be critical to business performance in the 1990s and beyond. The first section, **Recruitment and Training**, examines the challenges to traditional personnel management which are being posed by changes in demography, culture and competitiveness. Paul Johnson discusses the *demographic time-bomb* that is triggering this process. The ageing and shrinking of the population in the industrialised countries is changing the structure of the workforce, depleting the stock of young, skilled workers. As a result companies will have to redouble their efforts to find and keep the personnel they need.

In this changing environment, personnel managers will play an increasingly important role. Leonard Peach draws on his extensive experience as a personnel manager over three decades and in two very different organizations (IBM and the National Health Service) to delineate some of the problems and complexities that will confront personnel managers in the future. He outlines some potential strategies that involve not just the personnel departments, but a firm's entire structure.

Leslie Hannah examines the role played by British culture and institutions, particularly its public schools and universities, in hindering the recruitment of the most talented individuals to business. Armed with recent original data, he suggests some answers to the question of whether elite snobbery, the *cult of the amateur*, and the old boy network are things of the past. To be successful in human resource management, firms will have to *work smarter* as well as harder, employing a wider variety, and subtler range, of personnel strategies. Steve Shirley examines current definitions of work-time, and urges a redefinition of full-time and part-time, and a greater emphasis on alternatives – flexitime, working from home – made possible by a shift towards services, and the growth of information technology.

New and constructive approaches to human resources also involve issues seldom considered in the past. Richard Caruso, for example, discusses the costs of training new recruits who soon leave the company, and investigates the alternative strategy of a *mentoring culture*. In the process, he offers a closer analysis of what constitutes *mentoring*, and how the mentoring process should be redefined and actively deployed in order that practicing managers can capitalise on its usefulness as an important part of a company's human resource strategy. Part I concludes with an examination of the training and development of management by David Guest, Riccardo Peccei and Patrice Rosenthal. Using both a theoretical framework and hard evidential analysis, they find that management development has been undervalued but also note some signs of change, however.

In Part II, **Organization and Human Resources**, we look at some *organizational* problems. A key issue for Western business organizations is quality – which the Japanese have made a source of competitive advantage. Quality involves service as well as production, targeting customers and being prepared to adapt responsively to their requirements – in short, the establishment of a quality culture within the firm. Stephen Hill demonstrates that such total quality management demands a new appreciation of human resources, both in recruiting employees of the requisite merit, and in engaging them in the struggle for quality.

Eamonn Walsh describes some of the changes now taking place in management accounting. The refinement of that profession's analytical tools includes a greater appreciation of, and sensitivity to, the many variables related to human resources.

Ian Angell argues that a proper appreciation of the importance of human resources is also, paradoxically, vital in planning a company's information technology (IT) system. Businesses must not expect IT to supplant human resources. Moreover, organizational information systems must be designed with sensitivity to the broader human issues, so that IT strategy may be successfully integrated with corporate strategy.

The importance of integrating corporate strategy and a strategy for human resources is a theme which is continued by Greg Clark. He argues that the new personnel management models of the 1980s are already out of date as turbulent conditions in product-markets combine with a growing skills requirement. Companies must achieve flexibility at the same time as retaining valuable human assets. Greg Clark suggests profit-related pay as a potentially important strategic tool.

Christopher Huhne examines further the relationship between profit-related pay and company performance. He argues that profit-sharing fosters good performance and examines the economic consequences of profit-sharing to explain such performance. In particular, Christopher Huhne highlights improved motivation and management as the most enduring cause of increased profitability in profit-sharing companies.

Simon Taylor examines the surprising success of the John Lewis Partnership, and draws some optimistic conclusions about the potential benefits of co-operatism. This retail firm is owned by a trust on behalf of its employees, but retains the strong management structure necessary to avoid the pitfalls of *excessively ideological* co-operatives, which have failed in the past. This balance between the needs of running a business and co-operative ownership is not only more humane but has brought financial benefits to the firm: high staff morale and low staff turnover have led to greater productivity and better customer service.

The final chapter of the book takes a constructive look ahead. Richard Caruso argues that a firm's human resources should be considered as capital – *social capital* – comparable to financial capital, and subject to similar classifications. He distinguishes between *debt* and *equity* social capital, for example. The rise of high technology in modern industrial society, which demands that firms rely more upon the expertise of their personnel, underpins his case for qualitative and quantitative analysis and measurement of social capital as a precious resource.

RECRUITMENT AND TRAINING

3

Population Ageing and Employment Policies

Paul Johnson

Introduction

Human resources – workers, managers, customers and consumers – are the driving force behind the growth of modern economies. In the developed world we are used to thinking of these human resources as being readily, almost automatically available. Economic expansion in the twentieth century has been promoted by a consistent but moderate increase in the population, which has allowed just enough restocking of the labour market and just enough increase in consumer demand to provide a continuing stimulus to economic activity. But changes in the stock of human resources do not always have such benign effects, as the link between rapid population growth and endemic malnutrition in many third world countries shows. And over the next three to four decades demographic trends will also cause grave economic problems for the advanced economies. The problem will not be too many people but too few.

Between now and 2040 the working population of the European Community is projected to fall by 20 per cent – there will be forty five million fewer workers, forty five million fewer taxpayers – while the number of pensioners and infirm elderly people will increase significantly. This ageing and shrinking of the populations of Western Europe (already underway) is historically unprecedented, and so all predictions about its economic effects must be qualified by some degree of uncertainty. Yet we can be sure that the economic impact will be profound, with major changes occurring in the labour market, in social security mechanisms and fiscal burdens, and in the structure of demand.

This chapter examines the impact of this inexorable demographic change for business, and suggests how companies will have to change their attitudes and policies towards employment, training and retirement. First, let us explain briefly why our population is ageing and declining in size.

What is population ageing?

The demographic facts are quite straightforward: in industrial societies the proportion of old people in the population is increasing and the proportion of people of normal working age is falling. This shift is a consequence of two complementary processes, an increase in life expectancy and a decrease in fertility.

Improvements in life expectancy have been one of the major social achievements of the developed economies since the Second World War – the result of better nutrition, housing, public health and medical services. Between 1950 and 1980 average life expectancy at birth in the OECD countries rose by more than eight years for women and almost six years for men; life expectancy has also increased at higher ages, so that more seventy year olds now survive to eighty, and more eighty year olds live to ninety. However, these gains are not the primary cause of population ageing, which rather results from our failure to produce enough children.

Since 1950 the birth rate has been falling throughout Western Europe and North America. After the post-war *baby boom* came the *baby bust* of the late 1960s, 1970s and 1980s, when having children went out of fashion. Today in the European Community only the Republic of Ireland is increasing its population, while German, Italian and Danish birth rates have slumped so dramatically that on average every three couples now produce only four children altogether. Although fertility rates are not expected to remain this low indefinitely, few demographers believe they will return to the replacement level in the near future. The projections used in this chapter are taken from a recent OECD study which adopts mid-range estimates of future fertility and mortality rates, and so are a *best guess* at population trends in developed countries up to the year 2050.[1]

Even if these projections turn out to be too pessimistic, and fertility does return to something approaching the replacement rate by the year 2000 or shortly after, there will nevertheless be an enormous transitional problem by the third decade of the next century as the post-war *baby boom* generation enters retirement and turns to the small cohorts of working age adults for economic support. One measure of the costs today's children may have to bear is given by the old age dependency

Figure 3.1 Old age dependency ratios

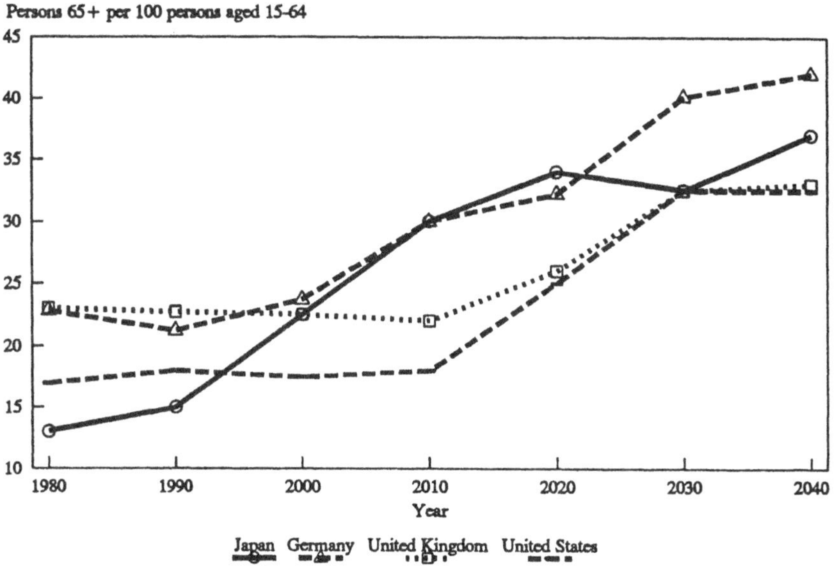

Persons 65+ per 100 persons aged 15-64

Japan Germany United Kingdom United States

ratio: the number of persons aged sixty-five and above to every hundred people aged fifteen to sixty-four. As figure 3.1 shows, this dependency ratio is already rising rapidly in Japan, will soon start upwards in Germany, and will accelerate from the second decade of the next century in Britain and the United States. As a result, the sixty-five and over age group will represent more than 20 per cent of the population in the developed countries by 2040, up from about one tenth in 1980. This rise in the proportion of elderly people will inevitably increase the economic demands that retired people place on those in work, which means that the tax contributions from workers and employers will need to rise sharply if the pension and welfare systems are to be sustained in their present forms. In Britain, the extra pension bill will increase the national insurance costs for each worker by around a half, so that total national insurance contributions will have to rise from the present level of 12.5 per cent of the wage bill to 18 per cent by 2030.[2] In 1989 it was projected that the payroll tax needed to sustain the West German pension system would have to rise from 18.5 per cent to around 42 per cent by 2030 (Schmahl, 1989, p. 143).

In all European countries employers directly bear a substantial proportion of these pension costs through their national insurance contributions. Thus this demographic change will sharply increase taxes on employment and production in the industrialised countries.

Figure 3.2 Index of working age population

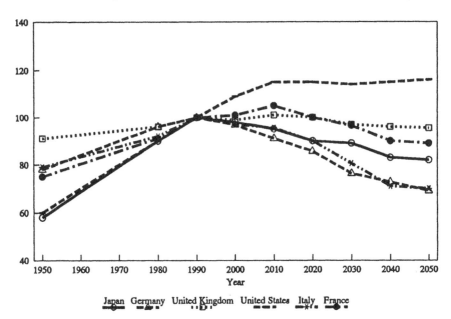

The economic costs of population ageing

This fiscal burden of an ageing population is only one small part of the overall economic cost. As figure 3.2 shows, the leading industrialised countries will have to adjust to very significant changes in their labour force over the next half century.

For each country, the working population in 1990 has been set equal to 100 so that future populations can be compared with this benchmark figure. In each of these countries the working population increased over the period 1950-90, at rates between 10 per cent (in Britain) and 80 per cent (in Japan). Three trends are apparent in the future:

1)   In the United States the working population will continue to grow for the next twenty years, after which it will stabilise at a level 15 to 18 per cent above the 1990 figure;

2)   In France and Britain the number of people of working age will be stable until 2020, after which it will fall fairly slowly;

3)   In Germany, Italy and Japan the working population is already declining and by 2050 these countries will have a potential workforce far smaller than that of today. In the case of unified

Germany the fall will be truly precipitate, from 53.5 million in 1990 to 36.9 million by 2050. This projected decline is greater than the *total* population of former East Germany.

All developed countries will need to adjust both labour and product markets to the novel conditions of stable or declining populations. Higher real incomes will partly offset the effects of fewer consumers, but in some market sectors, such as housing, demographic pressures will clearly have a depressive effect. In countries such as Germany and Italy the population is projected to decline substantially faster than the housing stock depreciates. In other market sectors, the change in the age structure of the population, together with an increase in the wealth of older people, will alter the age distribution of consumer demand. The booming teenage and young adult market of the 1960s and 1970s is a thing of the past, and the new growth area will be people in later middle age, a segment hitherto seldom targeted in marketing campaigns.

This change in the age structure of people under retirement age will also profoundly affect the workings of the labour market. In 1988 there were 800,000 sixteen year olds in the British population. Today there are 100,000 fewer, and by the end of 1992 there will be barely 600,000 people of school leaving age. Meanwhile, the number of workers in their late forties and fifties will rise sharply as the *baby- boomers* move into mature middle age. This shift is of potential importance since it is generally believed that younger workers are more flexible and have better and more recent training than older workers.

Not all people between fifteen and sixty-four are in employment. More young people are spending longer in higher education, and many women leave the labour force because of child-care and other family responsibilities. As a result, the actual labour force is considerably smaller that the working age population. A recent development in retirement practice – the concept of *early retirement* – has further reduced the size of the workforce. As figure 3.3 shows, the labour force participation rates for men aged fifty-five to sixty-four have fallen sharply since the mid 1960s in all the leading industrial countries except Japan (Guillemard, 1989, p. 168).

Since the fifty-five to sixty-four age group will become a larger share of the population over the next ten to fifteen years, the decline in its labour force participation will mean that the actual labour force will decline more rapidly in many countries than will the overall working-age population. Labour in industrial countries will become an increasingly scarce resource, a change that will require new attitudes and practices on the part of both governments and employers.

Figure 3.3 Labour force participation: Males 55-64 years old

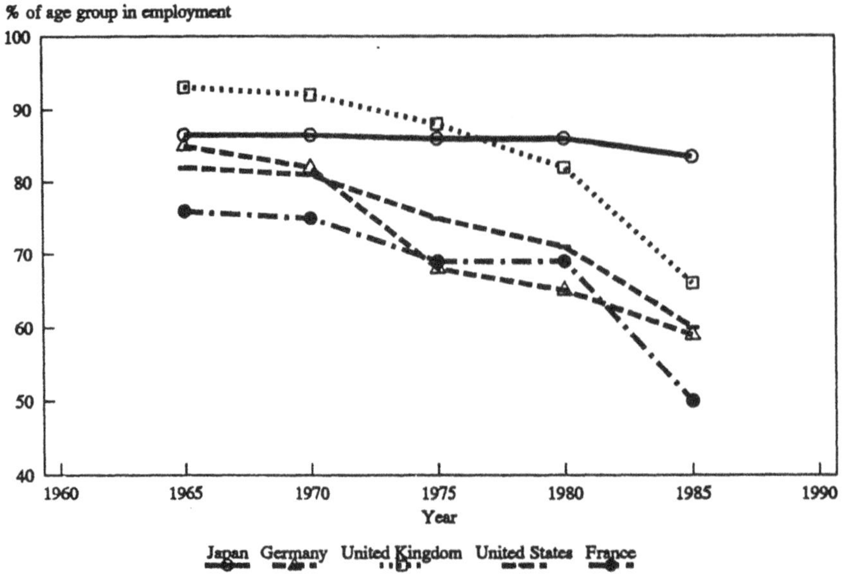

% of age group in employment

Employer responses to population ageing: The need for radical new thinking in personnel management practices

How *new* will these attitudes and practices need to be? Can the problem be solved by limited wage increases, juggling with bonus schemes and the offer of more tax-free perks? Will human resource managers be able to continue with *business as usual?* This seems unlikely.

Since the first oil price shock of 1974, the Western economies have experienced a prolonged period of general labour surplus, but demographic change will reverse these labour market conditions. Already a shortage of juvenile labour is apparent in much of Western Europe, which will lead to a general labour shortage by the end of the 1990s. This unprecedented demographic shock cannot be accommodated simply by tinkering with existing personnel management practices. What is needed is a new way of thinking, a paradigm shift, in human resource management. The most obvious example will be in the area of early retirement.

Over the last fifteen years, early retirement schemes have enabled employers to shed older workers with minimal political or trade union protest, while giving relatively well-off older workers a chance to opt for increased leisure at a younger age. Little effort has been put into providing training for older workers. Although industrial psychologists have known for thirty years or more that the productivity of older workers is in most occupations not significantly different from that of younger workers, many employers continue to assume that older workers are less productive.

The British government has already launched efforts to raise the pension entitlement age, which will tend to discourage companies from promoting early retirement. Labour shortage may be an even more important influence in this regard. Service sector companies, such as the supermarket chain Tesco in Britain and the Travelers Insurance Company in the United States, are already actively recruiting older people to fill the part-time and temporary vacancies formerly taken by juvenile or casual workers. Travelers Insurance found that the performance of it own retirees in temporary jobs was far superior to that of staff supplied by temporary employment agencies, and since 1985 the company has been holding *un-retirement parties* to expand enrolments in its *Job Bank* of older workers willing to undertake temporary employment. Travelers has also found, to its surprise, that many retirees are willing to be retrained in the use of new technologies, and that this training takes no longer than for younger workers. A senior vice-president of the company reports that:

> The return on our training investment has been substantial. Far from being wasteful – the common attitude towards spending money to train older workers – this program has yielded a productive group of people not otherwise available to us at any cost. (Libassi, 1988, pp. 350-360)

But such examples are exceptional; it will not be easy to reverse deeply entrenched personal and corporate attitudes to the employment of older workers. In Britain, figure 3.4 shows, the decline in labour force participation for men over sixty-five, which has been particularly rapid in recent years, is part of a long-run trend stretching back 100 years. Even in the period of acute labour shortage after the Second World War, older men withdrew from employment in ever increasing numbers despite intensive propaganda from the government to persuade both employers and workers that retirement should be postponed. Why are these patterns of retirement behaviour so difficult to change?

To manage their internal labour markets and secure the long-term loyalty of essential staff, many employers have established an earnings gradient in which pay is related to age. Since the marginal product of most workers does not seem to increase much above the age of fifty and in some cases declines, the profitability of workers tends to fall beyond middle age, and the incentive for the employer to remove the worker, usually by means of an early retirement deal, is strong. Rapid clear-out

Figure 3.4 Labour force participation rates: Males in England and Wales

Total population   Over-65 population

of older workers also ensures that promotion prospects for younger workers can be maintained. Although this is perhaps a caricature of the logic behind current personnel management practices, it is not a wholly fanciful description. Earnings gradients and early retirement are an important part of personnel policy today, and their removal would necessitate a major reconsideration of the way in which labour forces are managed.

For the individual, earnings gradients and early retirement also seem to make sense. Because so many occupational pension schemes define their benefits in relation to final salary (rather than life-time contributions), many workers do best when their salary is maximised in their final years of employment. This pattern can be achieved by a remuneration system based upon an age-related earnings gradient, and a labour contract that offers early retirement rather than demotion to a lower-paid job. At present it is not in the interest of either employers or workers to alter this system.

However, general labour shortage, and intense competition for skilled younger workers will make the continued employment of older workers essential. If employers are to make use of older workers' skills, and if the employees are to be willing to go on working, it will not be enough to offer minor cash incentives for the over fifty-fives. Instead there must be a major re-organization of the promotion and remuneration structures by which large employers today organize their internal labour markets (see chapter 4).

Furthermore, if older workers are to be encouraged to continue in employment (though not necessarily in their prime career job), they will need to be trained and retrained throughout their working life. The provision of training, even for juveniles, is hardly one of British industry's success stories, and almost no attention has been given to the particular problems of training older workers. Perhaps the promise of continual retraining throughout an extended working life can be used as an incentive to preserve employee loyalty and restrict labour turnover at a time when competition among employers for labour will become more intense.

Increasingly this competition will occur on a Europe-wide basis, which does not bode well for low-wage British employers. The generally low level of skill among the British workforce, which is compounded by a lack of in-service training, will be exacerbated as skilled staff are poached away by high-wage industries on the continent. As the pace of technological change quickens, constant retraining of the workforce will become more necessary. However, British employers will have scant incentive to bear the private cost of such training if the workers then carry their enhanced human capital to Germany or Italy where, because of a declining population, they can command much higher wages.

This combination of demographic pressure and technological change should encourage employers to reverse the move towards flexible labour contracts which has been so pronounced over the last decade. Businesses now need to consider how to develop effective long-term labour contracts that will guarantee a suitable return on the employer's investment in training. In Germany a return to formal apprenticeships for juveniles is already being discussed, as a means to prevent hectic labour mobility and wage inflation in the juvenile labour market. But since labour shortages will increase the demand for older workers, new ways need to be found to tie the middle-aged worker to the firm, so that mid-career retraining will be fully capitalised by the employer.

Here we should perhaps look at employment practices in Japan, where long-term (often life-time) welfare and housing benefits are used to tie the worker to the firm, and so ensure both employee loyalty and wage stability. A move towards long term employment contracts would be a fundamental challenge to current Western personnel management policies, which are geared to maximising labour force flexibility. Under conditions of abundant labour, flexible labour contracts are the least cost option, but they impose enormous public and private costs when workers, particularly skilled workers, are scarce.

Conclusion

In the relatively near future, labour shortages in the developed economies, particularly of skilled younger workers, will increase the bargaining power of labour, drive up labour costs and force employers to adjust their employment practices, particularly in relation to older workers and retirement. These adjustments will require a good deal of thought and planning, and some conscious re-orientation of the expectations of both employers and employees. If the adjustments are not made, the rising costs of labour among the shrinking populations of Western Europe and Japan will intensify the competitive advantage of third world economies, which will experience an expansion of their workforce and a decline in the relative size of their dependent child population in the early years of the next century. In the developed economies labour is a declining resource; we can no longer afford to waste it.

4

Excellence in Personnel Management

Leonard Peach

A few years ago, if I had been asked to analyse *excellence in personnel*, I might have felt restricted by the fact that my direct experience in personnel management, though covering every facet of the field, had for more than a quarter century been confined to one company, IBM. Now, however, my three and a quarter years with the National Health Service have more than made up for this deficiency.

Comparisons between these two great organizations are bound to be unfair. IBM has a record of some seventy-five years of excellent management, finely tuned over that entire period, with a dominant father figure, T J Watson, who *reigned* for about forty years and left his mark upon the business. The National Health Service is just discovering management after forty-five years and has experienced little consistency in that time. In my short span with the National Health Service under a single government, I had three Secretaries of State, three Ministers of Health, three Junior Ministers and three Spokesmen in the Lords. On average every senior post changed every year. In IBM UK Limited between 1965 and 1985 we had one managing director.

Nothing illustrates the rich tapestry of personnel management better than a speedy comparison between these two organizations. IBM had no unions; the National Health Service has forty-two. In IBM there is a tradition of full employment; the National Health Service is associated with putting out to tender some 170,000 jobs which substantially reduced the workforce. In one organization employment security is seen as vital to successful change; in the other insecurity is seen as a method of producing change.

In IBM management reigns supreme; the final choice of candidates rests with the line managers who have a great deal of discretion to use pay to reward and strengthen motivation. In the National Health Service, the appointment panel remains predominant at higher levels (in theory the senior manager receives what the panel disposes), and pay is decided centrally.

IBM's value system – based on respect for the individual, customer service and excellence – has been understood and reinforced for many years; in the National Health Service such a value system is just emerging. In IBM there is high pay. IBM has established appeal systems which must take no more than a fortnight to produce a resolution; in the National Health Service resolution of similar issues may take up to five years.

Despite these significant differences, both organizations have an employee commitment which does them credit. There is excellence in personnel management at the National Health Service. A good example of this is the professionalism with which it handled the closure of certain mental institutions and the associated staff redeployment. Another is the handling of the nursing clinical grading structure which promoted only about a 10 per cent dissatisfaction rate among employees – a level that most personnel managers in industrial corporations would be happy to see result from any job evaluation scheme. Thus we must be careful not to confuse excellence with reputation.

The clients of the personnel department: the chief executive, the management, the employees, the shareholders and the public at large will all have different ideas of what is meant by *excellence* in personnel management. They will all make judgements based on self-interest, but they will have different touchstones or measurements, depending on the service received, history, time and stage of development of the enterprise. David Lewin has done a considerable amount of work on the role of personnel in the various stages of business development and is shown in table 4.1.There are life cycle effects in personnel management. Another personnel director told me that he has been unable to recruit senior managers because his company is widely regarded as being in decline. As a result, his promotion policy has become entirely internally based and he has given young managers opportunities they would not have had in a mature enterprise.

Personnel managers never fully solve problems. They simply create new – and, we hope, smaller – ones. In solving IBM's manpower shortages of the 1980s, we created an environment in which employees aged over fifty had little hope of promotion. By redundancies and distribution of incentives to produce early retirement we have now produced a climate in which many members of that age group are looking forward to an enhanced pension, a golden handshake and early retirement. But times change. In the future British companies will need

Table 4.1 Business life cycle*

	Start up	Growth	Maturity	Decline
Selection, promotion and placement	Recruit best technical / professional talent. Entrepreneurial style.	Recruit adequate mix of qualified workers. Management succession planning. Manage rapid internal labour market movements.	Encourage sufficient turnover to minimize lay-offs and provide new openings. Encourage mobility as reorganizations shift jobs around.	Plan and implement work force reductions and reallocations. Transfers to different businesses. Early retirement.
Appraisal	Appraise milestones linked to plans for the business: flexibility.	Linked to growth criteria, eg, market share, volume unit cost reduction.	Evaluate efficiency and profit margin performance.	Evaluate cost savings.
Rewards	Salary plus large equity position.	Salary plus bonus for growth targets, plus equity for key people.	Incentive plan linked to efficiency and high profit margins.	Incentive plan linked to cost savings.
Management development	Minimum until a critical mass of people in business, then job related.	Good orientation programmes for fast start ups. Job skills. Middle-management development.	Emphasis on job training. Good supervisory and management development programmes.	Career planning and support services for transferring people.
Labour/employee relations	Set basic employee relation philosophy and organization.	Maintain labour peace, employee motivation and morale.	Control labour costs and maintain labour peace. Improve productivity.	Improve productivity. Achieve flexibility in work rules. Negotiate job security and employment adjustment policies.

The major human resource strategic categories and the Business Life Cycle (adapted with permission from Professor D Lewin, Columbia University).

to make maximum use of their mature employees. Personnel management, by being successful in the 1980s, has created a climate which is totally inappropriate for the demography of the 1990s (see chapter 3). Now we have to find new methods of retraining and motivating a mature population, many of whom feel that they should be allowed to retire early with a golden handshake. In their view, personnel managers have acted inconsistently.

In short, because the actions of personnel managers necessarily vary with the nature of specific problems – the state of development of the business, and fluctuations in the economy – over time we may appear to be inconsistent. It is crucial therefore that personnel managers provide sound explanations for their adopted strategies. The very complexity of the personnel function demands effective communication otherwise it can damage human resource managers.

Strategic personnel management insists that we pull against the pendulum. When times are good, line managers wants to give away the shop, *Keep production going at all costs*. Witness how British managers frequently allow earnings to rise faster than inflation. When times are bad the reaction can be equally pronounced – *taking on the trade unions*. As a result the natural pull of personnel directors is towards the centre, preventing wild oscillations which will ultimately have to be paid for. These are unpopular views, which have won a reputation for being over-cautious.

Add to this the paradoxes of personnel management – for example the need to offer substantial payoffs to those who have not served the company well, whilst retaining dedicated employees who have made themselves indispensable, but would dearly like to go. Add again the susceptibility of the personnel profession to fad and fashion, and the complexity of personnel management is revealed.

It is not my purpose to deal with external factors that influence the power base of personnel. I will simply note that labour relations, law and government regulations may lead to a wide variation of results. Some personnel directors shine in moments of crisis. IBM's personnel department was at its most visible (and some might say, at its best) at the time of the 1977 ACAS enquiry on union recognition. The British government's attempts at pay control in the 1970s also produced moments of glory for personnel departments that sought to mitigate that legislation's effects on their companies. Laws that reduced the incidence of crisis by changing power relationships in favour of employers also weakened the impact of personnel directors on organizations; this has been the story of some companies in the 1980s.

In short, it is the nature of personnel management itself which contributes to its image – internal or external. It is not difficult to see why chief executives, line managers, and employees are sometimes confused by the actions of personnel managers. Further, since personnel frequently sponsors difficult and often unpopular causes, such as equal opportunity in sex and race, it is especially difficult for it to present an image of excellence.

How can personnel project an image of quality?

In the 1950s and 1960s many personnel managers argued that all would be well if only personnel management had its place on the board. Board representation undoubtedly helps, by establishing a power base from which the personnel function can be influential. But it needs to be accompanied by other measures, notably a clear understanding with the chief executive and the top management team of the role which personnel will play in the company. Given the variety of influences on an organization, this understanding needs to be re-examined from time to time to ensure its relevance. The role of personnel may be clarified by a simple management-by-objectives approach between the chief executive and the personnel director, or by the formulation of an approved personnel plan. Some companies, including IBM, define *critical success factors:* objectives identified as crucial for overall company and departmental performance.

Critical success factors have the advantage of embracing the entire senior management team, providing a clear understanding of the main tasks of the functional heads and their interdependence. The *critical success factors* of IBM UK Limited are listed below. They signal a need for overall organizational change and the direction of that change.

Critical success factors (key objectives): *IBM UK Company*[1]

1) To change the company culture to one where delegation is maximised and all managers implement the correct level of risk taking and accept accountability for outcomes.

2) To understand constantly changing customer, and potential customer, needs and provide competitive solutions to satisfy these.

3) To develop and deploy IBM's and its business associates' skills, to transform IBM UK into, and manage it as, a *solution* company.

4) To manage workloads effectively.

5) To improve customer service and relationships: both direct from IBM and via our business associates.

6) To maintain the external good perception of IBM's contribution to the United Kingdom.

7) To organize and manage our people for high morale and motivation.

8) To have an effective management and control system to ensure that IBM UK achieves its business plan whilst providing a balanced performance on the seven *critical success factors* as above.

The *Critical success factors* for the IBM personnel function are as follows:

Critical success factors: Personnel function[2]

1) To keep the employee-manager relationship.

2) To meet IBM's stated compensation objectives.

3) To protect full employment.

4) To promote and maintain excellent people management.

5) To facilitate the management of differences whilst cultivating the fact that IBM is one company.

6) To promote the physical, mental and social well-being of all employees.

7) To progressively evolve IBM's employment practices and structures.

8) To provide education programmes to meet planned skill requirements.

9) To promote and maintain a credible, capable and effective personnel function.

10) To promote and maintain realistic and participative communication.

Points 1, 3 and 4 on the personnel department's *critical success factors* would have appeared on any similar chart for the past twenty-five or thirty years. More important are the changes taking place under points 2, 5, 7 and 8. In compensation we are seeking to reinforce delegation. Under 5, whilst preserving single status, we are recognising the different needs of the employed groups. (I emphasised the *mature* group earlier.) Under 7 we are moving away from the paternalistic relationships of the past, by allowing employees more choice in the nature of their employment with the company (eg, short term contract or permanent employment). Whilst education has always been one of IBM's strengths, point 8 recognises that recruitment will be highly competitive in the 1990s; we must now be able to sell continuous education to graduates who are becoming increasingly discerning on this topic.

The agreement between personnel and senior management on these critical success factors provides the contract which makes our future action comprehensible, acceptable and excellent. Debates on these topics have been particularly vigorous within the IBM personnel function, which views itself as the guardian of traditional corporate values: (*The Heritage*), and is now struggling to come to terms with changes it must support and advocate. Clearly a well defined value system may be helpful, but if it conflicts with business realities it may be detrimental.

Within IBM, the influence of personnel managers is enhanced by a process termed *non-concurrence*, or the *contention system*, whereby a particular function can object to a specific policy initiative. Personnel also has a strong base because of its influence on *patronage* within the organization. Because the personnel function has a commanding influence over executive pay and placement, personnel has little need to complain about its access to the *King's* ear and its power position within the patronage system.

Importance of Good Data

Most important of all is the existence of good data and information with which personnel can argue its case. Arguments cannot be won, plans cannot be formulated, without good information (see chapter 2). A lack of information is a major problem within the National Health Service, which one observer described as being 'awash with data but lacking in management information'. When I wanted to discover the national labour turnover of nurses, it cost £100,000 worth of a management consultant's time. The figure turned out to be 10 per cent of the qualified workforce: 30,000 out of 300,000 qualified nurses. The nursing unions immediately took up the cry '30,000 nurses a year are leaving the National Health Service'. Of course no one had the slightest idea how many nurses had left in the previous year, or in the ten years before that. In the late 1980s, amid all the shouts about morale and implementation of the clinical grading structure, labour turnover was down to 9 per cent, with a saving of £40 million in training costs and, more important, 3,000 less recruits needed in the 1990s. The National Health Service has discovered the words *retention* and *return*.

Only by the accumulation of relevant information can personnel win its battles. In IBM there were many debates in the 1960s in which the finance director was loaded with highly qualified information but personnel could only say 'we think that...'. If the *peasants* are revolting, we have to know how many are revolting, how revolting they are, why are they revolting, and whether there is a trend. Then we may win the battle for the appropriate solution. Personnel must have both numeracy and social skills, and also the measurements to assess the quality of the organization's *people* performance. The saying 'if you can't measure it, you can't manage it' is just as relevant to personnel as any other branch of management. In recent years the LSE Business Performance Group has successfully developed innovative techniques to assist personnel managers in this regard (see chapter 2 and Bradley and Taylor, 1992).

To make sense of the complexities of personnel management, one needs to communicate to the workforce on a regular basis what is happening and why it is happening, explaining and reconciling inconsistencies with previous statements. Good communication can minimise or pre-empt the challenge to significant changes in business direction. As personnel directors, we can enhance our own image and explain our part in the changes we are seeking, ensuring that we are identified with the nature of the change and its intent. However, if we are incompetent as managers or personnel professionals, then the contradiction between our communications and our actions will undermine our credibility. Personnel directors cannot advocate high standards of management for other functions without achieving them within their own departments.

In sum, there are several requirements for excellence in personnel management: representation on the board, a clearly understood role and mission, a reinforcing management system, intelligent use of patronage, good information systems, a strong hand in communications, and clear competence in personnel management.

Resources are a critical consideration. The ability of a personnel department to discharge its agreed functions is limited by its strength and capability. Some personnel directors essentially restrict themselves to acting as the personnel managers for the top management of the organization; they discharge this responsibility with minimum staff and a substantial use of headhunters. In IBM, Marks and Spencer, and other *excellent* organizations, resources are between one and two personnel people per hundred employees, depending on responsibilities. In the National Health Service it was 0.3. Therefore, in a hospital with some 3,000 employees one would expect to find a personnel staff of nine conducting their activities against a backdrop of a labour turnover rate in the region of 25 per cent.

With limited resources and restricted roles it is difficult for personnel managers to be excellent. Furthermore, without a strong internal *management development* department, the chances of achieving and maintaining excellence are also remote. Necessary change is produced by perspiration and persistence, by using all the organization's communication and training mechanisms reinforced by appropriately modified policies.

Conclusion

Excellence in personnel management means identifying with the short and long term aims of the core business, meeting the standards of customer satisfaction which typify other successful functions, while using communication mechanisms to keep employees' expectations realistic. Excellent personnel managers will recognise conflicts and paradoxes, and the need to choose among objectives; they will be ready to explain their choices, and any perceived inconsistencies. They must be prepared to recommend a choice which suits the organization's long term needs rather than be bulldozed by short term advantage. At times they must be prepared to stand alone. I remember in the 1960s listening to personnel managers on public platforms indicating that they had agreed with their shop stewards that management should communicate with its workforce only through them. I do not remember voices of protest being raised.

In the 1990s excellence in personnel management will be determined by the ability to recruit and handle a workforce at the two extremes of age, the under twenty-fives and the over fifties; to achieve the economic benefits of equal opportunities advanced more by need than by legislation; to recognise the importance of training and continuous development; and to expand the flexible workforce in employment conditions and in physical location.

Personnel can win a reputation for excellence at both company and national levels. Problems become challenges and opportunities, and there is nothing like the kaleidoscope of management experience which one can enjoy in a life of personnel management. Tom Peters' prescription for excellence, from his book *Thriving on Chaos* based upon creating total customer responsiveness, pursuing fast-paced innovation, achieving flexibility by empowering people and learning to love change. Given the complexities and contradictions of personnel management, it would seem that the excellent personnel director is well qualified to become the chief executive of the future. Personnel managers should make a virtue of their *weaknesses:* the very nature of their work is a pursuit of excellence. Some will say that they will never catch it – but what an exciting chase it is!

5

Human Capital Flows and Business Efficiency

Leslie Hannah

'....for a long time I have felt that the contribution by businessmen to society is widely misunderstood and constantly maligned by those who should know better.' (Margaret Thatcher, speech to the Institute of Directors, 15 September 1976)

Business felt the whip of competition in the 1980s, but the pain was tempered by the feeling that, whatever happened in specific policy areas, Margaret Thatcher's government prized and respected the business leader's function in society. Such respect is not entirely new. Yet many commentators have remarked on the unusually strong anti-industrial, anti-enterprise or anti-business strands in British culture. Most notable is Martin J. Wiener's book, *English Culture and the Decline of the Industrial Spirit 1850-1980* (1981), which chronicles the development of gentlemanly anti-business ideals, their transmission through the public school and university systems, the myths of rural innocence lost in industrialised Britain, and the middle classes' persistent ambivalence towards science, innovation and entrepreneurship. Wiener writes:

'At the end of the day it may be that Margaret Thatcher will find her most fundamental challenge not in holding down the money supply or inhibiting government spending or even in fighting the shop stewards, but in changing this frame of mind. English history in the eighties may turn less on traditional political struggles than on a cultural contest between the two faces of the middle class.' (Wiener, 1981)

The natives were extremely agitated by this timely (and best selling) contribution to the debate on the British disease, but deeply divided in their reaction. Business leaders endorsed Wiener's thesis (Goldsmith, 1985). Many of them saw anti-business prejudice lurking not only among left-wing politicians, but also in the corridors of power, in the media and in the schools and universities. Others pointed out that this anti-business culture looked like those responsible for business failure shrugging off the blame onto others. Nonetheless, government ministers welcomed the cultural diagnosis of failure as enthusiastically as businessmen and claimed that their own pro-enterprise policies were the proper response to the need for changed cultural attitudes.

Opinion poll evidence, meanwhile, failed to show a grass roots alienation from industry – or to support Margaret Thatcher's hopes for a substantial change in attitudes. For most people, experience and the simple need to make a living produced simpler (and less easily ridiculed) views: according to the pollsters, industry and business were popular in the abstract, but were distrusted because of their perceived inability to deliver and sustain job security. Margaret Thatcher's emphasis on enterprise and self-reliance may even have created greater rather than less awareness of these shortcomings (Jowell *et al.*, 1987; Crewe, 1989).

Such evidence may have dented Wiener's thesis slightly, but the most devastating attacks on his interpretation of anti-business culture came from his fellow academics, whose institutions were under attack: by financial cuts from government as well as by words from Wiener (who held the universities responsible for transmitting Britain's anti-business culture), (McKendrick and Outhwaite, 1986; Rubinstein, 1988). Evidence showed the flimsiness of the alleged correlation between literary culture and businessmen's behaviour. After all, anti-business prejudices were just as powerful during Britain's heyday as the workshop of the world as in her twentieth century decline. Equally, the bitter socialist rhetoric of Brecht and the anti-Westernism of some Japanese novelists have not prevented their countries from enjoying modern economic miracles.

Wiener's critics even speculated on a reversal of his hypothesis, arguing that successful entrepreneurs have typically come from *out-groups* such as the Jews, Quakers, or immigrants. On this view the creative destruction of the established order by the socially disapproved businessmen is the main spring of economic progress, and establishment *support* for business would be its death knell. Certainly British aristocrats appear to have adopted *bourgeois* business pursuits more enthusiastically than their more conservative, agrarian continental counterparts, without noticeably boosting British growth.

The inconclusive debate left policymakers with no proper guidance based on accurate analyses of the dynamics of cultural change and its potential effects. But that did not necessarily prevent their policies from being effective. How far *has* Britain been culturally transformed by the changes promoted by men of affairs?

The difficulty of tying down generalisations about national cultural attitudes allowed the academic nitpickers a boisterous field-day of inconclusive debate. Yet some of the points they were debating *can* be reduced to measurable and testable propositions. There is a wealth of historical material on the social and cultural background of British businessmen and on how they differ from their overseas counterparts. It is also possible to use more recent biographical data on businessmen to assess how far things have changed in the 1980s.

Information on business leaders' educational backgrounds is plentiful: in Britain's *old school tie* society, establishment figures are rarely reticent about their school, and social commentators have made the most of this. There are, for example, two common (though contradictory) cultural stereotypes of the public schools' impact on British business. In the older stereotype, which is part of the general left-wing critique of the British establishment, businessmen (and more particularly top managers and financiers) are born into the wealthier classes and educated at public schools *for* leadership positions, which they inherit (or wangle on the old boy network) rather than earn. Other observers, by contrast, see the public schools as a major force directing young men *away* from business careers, instilling a sense of the inherent superiority of other, more *gentlemanly* callings.

There is a great deal of variety among schools and in the same school at different times, and thus probably some truth in both views. It is correspondingly easy to *disprove* any generalisations: for example, evidence can be produced that many public schools in the postwar years have been more likely to recruit the sons of businessmen, to encourage boys to go into business and to educate them to as high a level in the sciences as they once did in the classics.

Views can easily change in the cut and thrust of the debate: indeed the stereotype I described as the left-wing view is perhaps best exemplified in the critical essays on *The Establishment* (1959), edited by the (then) left-wing historian Hugh Thomas; and the right-wing view in the same author's later pamphlet, published by the Thatcherite Centre for Policy Studies. We are evidently in something of a shifting quagmire when discussing British anti-business culture.

If one has to choose between the rival stereotypes of British culture, there is little doubt that the left-wing view is nearer to the truth. Countless surveys have shown the disproportionate representation of public school men in senior management positions in industry. Indeed from the 1920s through the 1940s, when the postwar generation of business leaders who figure in the early surveys were being educated, firms recruiting trainee managers often specified that they would primarily consider public school men of *character* or those with personal introductions and from good families (Acton Society Trust, 1956; Keeble, 1984). Open recruitment by merit was confined to a relatively small part of the business sector.

At the same time, there was sometimes a disdain for the academically inclined and particularly for the university graduate. Thus international comparisons of the higher education of businessmen typically show that directors of British companies were paragons of under-education. In the 1950s, only a third of top British businessmen had been to university – a level already exceeded in the business elites of major industrial competitors such as America, Germany, France and Japan *before the First World War* (Lazonick, 1986; Warren and Abegglen, 1955; Kaelble, 1985; Mannari, 1974). More up-to-date surveys suggest that, while the proportion of graduates in top management has slowly increased, Britain still lags behind other countries (Handy, 1987; Hall *et al.*, 1969, pp. 45-55). This was, moreover, not obviously a general failing of British society or education, for other elites became significantly more meritocratic and open than the business elite in the course of the twentieth century (Rubinstein, 1986).

There may be no connection between British business leaders' relative lack of (and unusually socially exclusive form of) education and their firms' poor economic performance. Business – like most callings – requires a good deal more than the effort and intelligence measured by university degree courses. Moreover, in comparison with those of other nations, British universities have played a different social and even educational role. Only in recent decades, for example, has it become *de rigueur* for bright upper-class children to attend university in Britain, while universities have traditionally been weak at vocational training (particularly business training).

There is no precise social and educational equivalent of the public school abroad, but other countries restrict access to business leadership position by parallel means, some of which are no more conducive than British public schools to the training needs of business. It could even be argued that the British practice of allowing bright and effective non-graduate employees to progress to top positions is a strength, whereas requiring degrees for entry to senior management positions (as in the British professions or most leading overseas businesses) is a damaging artificial barrier to the success of the ambitious.

Such views, usually honestly based on direct experience with single cases and reasoning from first principles, have been repeatedly advanced over the last hundred years by advocates for British avenues of promotion, social mobility and leadership recruitment. Certainly, while an under-valuing of education in modern technologically-advanced society can be extremely damaging, *credentialism* – excessive reliance on paper qualifications – can itself compromise meritocracy. But the fact remains that the flowering of the British system has coincided with economic decline relative to countries with other systems.

Britain can no longer be so sanguine. At the very least it has increasingly been recognised that the burden of proof rests on those wishing to defend the established system. Movement towards the more economically successful norms of Britain's overseas business competitors, it is hoped, may signal an improvement in the quality of British business leadership.

But how much actually changed in the 1980s? The networks of influence, the prestige of schools and universities, the nature of training and education, the ladders of promotion within large organizations -these change not by the month or the year, but by the generation. They have been extraordinarily stable, over many generations, in Britain. This country did not experience the upheaval of revolution or defeat in war that dislodged old entrenched elites and stimulated economic growth in much of continental Europe and Japan. Two Cambridge sociologists, Philip Stanworth and Anthony Giddens, illustrated British elite stability between 1905 and 1971 in their study of the chairmen of the largest industrial and commercial companies, (Stanworth and Giddens, 1974). They found that public school men, particularly those from top schools such as Eton or Harrow, were dominant throughout the period and there was only a gradual (and small) increase in the minority of chairmen who had attended universities.

The 1980s saw, it is true, a remarkable anti-establishment upheaval in the political world, as Margaret Thatcher's confidence and power were reinforced by political success. Many Old Etonians (who had long dominated Conservative cabinets) were passed over or dismissed by the Prime Minister, who distrusted their style and was determined to brook no opposition from the traditional grandees of the Conservative Party. Her actions provoked shocked establishment growls such as the remark attributed to her one-time Secretary of State for Defence, Francis Pym: 'The trouble is we've got a corporal at the top, not a cavalry officer'. As *The Guardian's* political correspondent observed, the Old Etonian, ex-Lancer Pym 'epitomised, in manner and class and cunning habit and squireish paternalism and innumerate dedication to the feel of politics rather than the facts of economics, everything that she wanted to defenestrate from the Conservative citadel' (Young, 1989, p. 331).

Margaret Thatcher made full use of her political power. But beyond the cabinet room her writ ran in company boardrooms only in the public sector, and even there its run was being rapidly reduced by privatisation.

Many journalists claimed that the whole cultural fabric of British business was turned upside down in the 1980s. *Business* magazine in 1989 was sure that 'A new class of managers has emerged from the ranks....The Young Turks had fewer hang-ups about status. Many had degrees or a professional qualification such as accountancy....the cult of the amateur was over' (*Business*, May 1989). But such claims had been made regularly since the war, without having much measurable impact on the composition of the business elite.

Researchers at the London School of Economics (LSE) have therefore taken a preliminary look at the changes between 1979 and 1989 in the career and educational backgrounds of chairmen of Britain's leading industrial and commercial companies. The results for the top fifty companies (shown in table 5.1) are striking. Far from confirming the relative stability of earlier studies, they show a marked acceleration of change in the background of the business elite. The most remarkable shift is in the secondary education of business leaders, a group formerly dominated by public school men. Today a majority of chairmen went to grammar schools or to schools maintained by the state. The top public schools showed a substantial loss in membership of the business elite. Eton, which in 1979 had educated the chairmen of five of the top fifty companies (paralleling its dominance in other areas of the establishment), could claim none of the top chairmen by 1989. The representation of public schools as a whole declined by more than half over the decade.[1]

The rising stars in the top boardrooms were the grammar school men; comprehensives were, of course, rare when this cohort of chairmen were schoolboys.[2] Some attended the famous direct grant schools, such as Manchester Grammar School, which during their era offered many free places and charged low fees; other chairmen came from local grammar schools in the state sector.

Typical of these new men is Sir Peter Walters, former chairman of Britain's largest company, British Petroleum. With just a light touch of the new elite's inverted snobbery, he describes his background as 'intelligent working class' (Goldsmith and Ritchie, 1987, p. 152): one of his grandfathers was a school teacher, another a police constable; his father joined Birmingham City Police Force at eighteen and became its youngest Chief Inspector at thirty-two. Walters himself was educated at King Edward High School in Birmingham, a direct grant school. Entering Birmingham University to read law, he switched within two weeks to the commerce degree. Like many who benefitted from the direct grant and grammar school system, he is unashamedly meritocratic and regrets the system's demise.

Table 5.1 Secondary education of the chairmen of the top fifty companies

	1979	1989
"Top" public schools*	9	1
Other public or fee-paying schools**	20	11
"Top" grammar schools***	4	8
Other grammar schools	5	12
Other maintained schools	9	15
Educated abroad	3	3
Total	50	50

* defined as the original "Clarendon" schools (Charterhouse*, Eton*, Harrow, Rugby*, Shrewsbury*, Winchester*, Westminster, Merchant Taylors' and St Paul's); only the asterisked schools were actually represented in our samples for 1979 and 1989.

** these are mainly members of the Headmasters' Conference and boarding schools. Two chairmen in 1979 and 1 chairman in 1989 came from lesser fee paying schools which were not members of the HMC.

*** schools listed as direct grant grammar schools by the Department of Education and Science or Scottish Education Department in 1964. Most were members of the Headmasters' Conference. These were mainly day schools which at the relevant time took a socially wider range of pupils, including many not paying fees, though they became fully independent and fee paying after 1974.

Note: information on educational background was traced for all but one of the chairmen in 1979 and all but three in 1989. E S Margulies (Berisfords) appeared in both years. He grew up in the Hasidic Jewish community of the East End and has been assumed to have attended an "other maintained school". Lord Hanson (Hanson Trust) attended a "public school" but we could not ascertain which; he has been counted as attending an "other public school". Lord King's early history is obscure; he "left school with no qualifications" and he has been assumed to have attended an "other maintained school".

Source: Top fifty companies by turnover as listed in the *Times 1000* for 1978-79 and 1988-89 (excluding Englehard which had no chairmen). Data on education from *Who's Who*, other similar directories, press clippings, libraries, and the subjects themselves. Research by Alison Sharp, London School of Economics.

Upward mobility was even possible from the less prestigious *other maintained* sector, which contributed fifteen chairmen in 1989 – six more than in 1979.

These changes should not be exaggerated: they are based on a small sample of the top fifty companies and, given the problems of state education in the 1970s and 1980s, may not be sustained. Yet, the apparent changes in the 1980s are greater than those recorded in previous studies of the business elite over the entire twentieth century.

This astonishing change can be interpreted in a variety of ways. One possibility is that the social elite and the wealthy (who traditionally sent their children to public schools) have recently become more alienated from business than in earlier decades. Just as at the end of the nineteenth century they reduced their exposure to the risk of farm landholdings in the agricultural depression, so they are now reducing their risks in business when it is exposed to the winds of world competition. This, however, seems implausible: for where is there now in the British economy to go, that is *not* suffering the winds of competition?[3] A more plausible interpretation is that whereas ex-public schoolboys could once get to the top through family influence, the *old school tie*, and their educational advantages, such influences have now declined, whether as a result of changing social ethics, widening educational opportunities for others or increased competition and professionalism in business. The public school men who are in top jobs now are, on this interpretation, much more likely than their predecessors to have obtained their position by merit. The private and state sectors are now represented at almost exactly the level of their relative sixth form sizes when these chairmen were young.[4]

Opportunities have increased for the more successful pupils from the state schools – often from modest, though still rarely from unskilled working class backgrounds – to climb to the top of the business ladder. The improvements in the state education system after the Second World War, and the effective recruitment of able school leavers and, more especially, of university graduates, have together created a more open career ladder in business.

That formal education (rather than merely traditional *character, enterprise* or *business genius*) is an important aspect of their success is clear from the chairmen of 1989 who attended the *other maintained schools*. On the whole these were *not City barrow boys:* undereducated geniuses rejected at eleven plus by grammar schools and too poor to pay public school fees. Many of these *other maintained* schools were highly selective and academic, some grammar schools in all but name. And these chairmen were clearly academically gifted: in fact, twelve out of fifteen of them went to university.

Overall changes in the university education of the 1989 chairmen (table 5.2) are less striking, but support the meritocratic interpretation. The increase in the proportion of business leaders attending university (already apparent in the earlier postwar decades) continued in the 1980s. Only thirteen of the top fifty chairmen of 1989 (mainly public school men and a few self-made men with no educational qualifications) did not attend university. Moreover, the precipitate decline in representation of the elite public schools has not been paralleled by the elite universities of Oxbridge[5] and London (which, for top businessmen,

Table 5.2 University education of the chairmen of the top fifty companies

	1979	1989
Oxford	5	11
Cambridge	14	5
London	4	4
Birmingham	2	5
Other British universities	3	8
Overseas universities	3	3*
No university education	19	14
Total	50	50

including Virgin Polytechnic, an institute with university status.

Sources: as Table 5.1. Sir Owen Green (BTR) is not counted as attending Oxford, for his university studies were brief, being interrupted by the War. Others for whom no information on university was available were assumed to have had no university education.

usually means the London School of Economics). Since the Second World War, rising state financial support has enabled these elite universities to recruit more on the basis of academic merit than wealth (certainly significantly more so than the fee-paying public schools.)

However Oxbridge and London no longer dominate the graduate playing field. The proportion of chairman educated at *other British* universities more than doubled in the 1980s. (These are established *redbrick universities* not the new *plateglass* foundations of the 1960s, which came too late for most of this generation of chairmen.) Birmingham University led the way. With its long tradition of industrially-inclined vocational courses, it produced as many of the 1989 chairmen as Cambridge.

These changes in the business elite in the 1980s no doubt have many causes. Mrs Thatcher can take the credit for some of the appointments: the top fifty companies of 1989 include half a dozen nationalised and recently privatised companies whose chairmen she and her ministers appointed or promoted at an earlier stage, and public school men were rare in this group. Yet most of the changes in the private sector cannot be explained in this way. These chairmen's links with the Prime Minister generally parallel those of Sir Owen Green, chairman of BTR, who remarked:

'I think you could say that I am an outsider. I am not in the Thatcher *mafia* and I am not a political animal. I am a supporter of Thatcherism, in the sense and to the extent that it has helped to bring about some necessary changes in the environment.'

(*Business*, May 1989, p. 52; see also Fay, *Business*, December 1988)

Even this connection is tenuous: Thatcherism's celebration of the virtues of the self-taught business genius pulling himself up by the bootstraps *paper* qualifications was hardly calculated to promote the changes we observe.

Thatcherism had an indirect effect, however. Some of the changes shown in tables 5.1 and 5.2 are the result of upheavals among the leading companies caused by the strong competitive pressures and restructuring of the 1980s Thatcher whirlwind. Some companies, such as BTR and Saatchi & Saatchi – relatively small in 1979 – appear only on the 1989 list, along with the privatised or about-to-be privatised companies. Other companies on the 1979 list, such as Amalgamated Metal and C.T. Bowring, were knocked off by the collapse of their markets in the 1980s, and they have not recovered their position since. Yet half the companies appear on both the 1979 and 1989 lists. Within this group there were also substantial personnel changes, suggesting that the move to meritocracy reflects shifts within companies and not just the changed composition of the top fifty.

It seems certain, moreover, that the foundations for such widespread changes were laid much earlier than the 1980s: when the business leaders in question were being recruited, trained and promoted. The average age of the chairmen of 1989 was fifty-nine. They had typically finished their education in the 1950s, and progressed through middle management positions in the 1960s and board promotions in the 1970s. These were decades of widening educational opportunity, but also, we are now prone to forget, of profound changes in attitudes both within and towards business. As the major continental European countries began perceptibly to overtake British living standards in the 1960s, social and cultural changes accelerated, stimulated by the increased contemporary perception of the national, industrial and personal importance of business success. Concretely this was reflected in the inauguration of business sections in the quality newspapers, and by the foundation (eighty years after the pioneering American business schools) of major new centres of business education like the London and Manchester Business Schools.

There may also have been an acceleration of changes in the wider cultural fabric of Britain (described by Wiener) that are less easy to convey, given the problems of generalisation about national culture. Anecdotally, I have the impression that such changes did have a tremendous effect on promotion procedures and professionalism within the leading British firms, but it is difficult to substantiate such an impression statistically. We can, however, observe the effects of these changes on the people that businesses were able to recruit, notably in the career choices of university graduates.

The small numbers of graduates among the postwar business elite suggest that in the first half of the twentieth century, when that generation were recruited, business careers were a minority taste at British universities. This is confirmed by the scattered contemporary statistics: possibly only a third of graduates then opted for careers in business (statistics in Sanderson, 1972; *Political and Economic Planning*, 1956). By the 1960s, however, the proportion of the (then much increased numbers of) university graduates opting for a career in industry and commerce reached two-thirds and it has since remained at about that level (*University Statistics*, vol 2; University Grants Commission, 1968-80). While the data is not strictly comparable, it seems, moreover, that the postwar enthusiasm of Japanese and German graduates for business careers may have been waning in the 1980s. Thus Britain's *relative* position could be improving even more rapidly than is implied by her own apparent shift in cultural attitudes – if that *is* what lies behind the changes.

There has been an equally remarkable transformation in the *quality* of British students who opt for careers in business. Not only do more students choose business-related university courses (engineering, accountancy or business management) but they are getting better A Level grades (University Grants Commission, *Annual Reports*, 1968-69/1987-88, *Statistical Supplements*). In the increasingly popular business-oriented courses *more* has certainly not meant *worse*.

There are clear indications, also, that the best students in *all* undergraduate disciplines, not just in those orientated to business, are showing more interest in business careers than they did earlier. Past questionnaire surveys used to uncover *reasons for going into business* that included failure in the civil service exams, or a poor degree: business was the choice only by default. Wiener quotes Margaret Drabble's novel *The Ice Age*, set in early 1960s Cambridge, to illustrate the survival of this view:

> 'It must be said that it never once crossed Anthony Keating's mind that he might get a job in industry ... He thought himself superior to that kind of thing: that kind of advertisement was aimed at bores and sloggers, not at men of vision like Anthony Keating.' (Wiener, 1981, p. 36)

This view was in fact already becoming obsolete in 1960s Cambridge, and it is now emphatically not the view of the brightest graduates, at least judging by their career choices. The increased output of British university graduates with first class honours since the war period has gone almost entirely to the business sector. Meanwhile, business has not recruited a higher proportion of graduates with third class honours or pass degrees (also produced in increasing numbers); these graduates have gone into the public sector, particularly local authorities.

The trend favourable to business is, moreover, now firmly established, with continuing success in business recruitment of first class honours graduates apparent in all recent decades. Not only has there been a revolution, it seems, but it is firmly rooted in evolutionary cultural and educational change. Firm foundations have been laid for a society in which graduates increasingly recognise the worth, challenge and rewards of a career in business, and business can draw on many of the brightest brains in their generation, making possible in the 1980s the final push towards a more meritocratic selection at the top.

These changes can be expected to benefit business efficiency in the 1990s, provided academic degree results reflect in some way the combinations of effort, intelligence and other factors which are also conducive to business success. Certainly those with first class honours were well-represented among the top company chairmen of 1989: James Prior of GEC (First in Estate Management from Cambridge), Maurice Saatchi of Saatchi & Saatchi (First in Sociology from London School of Economics), Sir Robert Haslam at British Coal (First in Electrical Engineering from Manchester), and Sir Christopher Hogg of Courtaulds (First in English from Oxford). Some of the new men of 1989 have also topped off their education with a postgraduate business degree: two (Hogg and the American R P Bauman of SmithKline Beecham) with a Harvard MBA, and one (Ian Vallance of British Telecom) with the equivalent from the London Business School.

Of course, most graduate chairmen (like most successful graduates elsewhere) obtained second class honours degrees. Further, indeed, the best *Seconds* among them were fully a match for the *Firsts:* this is as true in business as in most other callings. What is clear is that the relatively few Firsts – whose increased recruitment by business happens to be measurable – include a significant portion of the cream of their generation. Certainly recruiters for the large corporations, though careful to stress their search for the rounded individual, tend to favour the academically successful when making offers. They have for some decades looked for the same qualities as are reflected in the award of a First. Salary surveys show that firms – though often not knowing degree results when making an offer – in fact pay more to Firsts than to their other recruits; moreover, this differential persists in business salaries years later.

All the signs are, then, that the British business world is now substantially more meritocratic than it was a generation ago. The men at the helm of the top British businesses in the early 1990s are largely drawn from the intellectual cream. It is, moreover, clear that their successors in the late 1990s will also be drawn from an impressive pool of first-class talent. These trends alone will not necessarily make a great difference to the strategic performance of British companies in the increasingly competitive markets they now face – but they are encouraging.

6

The New Workforce

Steve Shirley

The workforce of the future has been much discussed, as has the use of part-timers, flexitime, and the distributed worker. These are important issues. Equally important, though neglected, is the need for a change in attitudes in British management, a change that will allow us to take greater advantage of the opportunities a *new workforce* could bring. Such change is essential if the West is to sustain growth. The 1990s can be seen as bringing problems – or opportunities.

The demise of traditionalism

Many organizations think it unsavoury or not quite right to employ people in anything but the traditional nine-to-five Monday to Friday slot. They force their employees to compete in the daily rat race and think this is the way God intended us all to work. The more *progressive* companies claim to have taken a fresh look and introduced flexitime. But how much freedom does this really give employees? Workers are generally constrained by a core day of, say, ten to three. In many cases their situation is probably reminiscent of the old joke 'I can start anytime I like before eight thirty and leave anytime I like after six.' This does not really tackle the problem we in the Western world are about to face.

Many aspects of the employment situation are changing: values, attitudes towards profit, the age and sex composition of the workforce. Employers will need to find a completely *new workforce* to fill the gaps in their staff caused by the so-called demographic time-bomb, which is about to explode (see chapter 3). During the 1990s demand for skilled workers will increase, not only in industries such as information technology (IT), but as a reflection of fundamental changes in the structure of *all* British organizations.

The demographic time-bomb will not explode overnight; it is on a slow, but steady, fuse. However, it will dry up our normal supply of young workers. Already, the birth rate in the United Kingdom is below replacement level, and the number of young people entering the labour market aged fifteen to twenty-nine will fall by 1.9 million or 14 per cent by 1996 (see chapter 3). To avoid the crippling effects of staff shortages, managers will have to look elsewhere for workers – or pay a premium for the scarce young people who are available.

New industries such as information technology, and old industries as well, are requiring increasing numbers of skilled workers, because of the proliferation of new technologies. These technologies have reduced companies' needs for manual workers, and increased their demand for highly skilled and trained staff. In recent years the growth in demand for skilled workers has been truly phenomenal, and it is likely to continue rising exponentially.

A still more fundamental force increasing demand for a *new workforce* is the change in operations and structure that will occur in most businesses during the next decade. As Britain becomes a truly advanced industrial nation, operating practices will move towards a more *service-oriented* culture. Business will move away from the present, classic, hierarchical structure, towards a completely new concept and form. Professor Handy identifies the structure which is likely to emerge in his excellent book, *The Age of Unreason.*

In its new form, a company will have three key elements:

1) A core of in-house managers

2) A non-permanent, less skilled operational group of *doers* such as temps and freelance typists

3) A huge group of consultants, who will provide new ideas, creativity and intellectual muscle that will be the basis of the new business environment

Such a system is considerably more flexible than the current *modus operandi*, and can produce a greater variety of results. The core in-house manager will be able to choose the flavour of the business and, most importantly, will be able to respond to changes in the business environment more rapidly and in more ways than are now possible. Consultants will be charged with adding value to their clients and not just providing a basic service. Such a business structure is highly dependent on skilled labour, and this is why British employers will need to consider ways of recruiting a *completely new workforce*. The new organization offers great opportunities for competitive advantage through increased flexibility.

Why worry about this change? The simple fact is that for the first time since the mid-1960s, employment will be a seller's market. Potential staff, not employers, will call the tune. The scarcity of employees will force a reassessment of our definition of a part-timer. (Such definitions have changed before. The Victorians, for example, would have considered today's nine-to-five routine part-time. They worked ten hours a day, and six days a week, with only five days off in a year.) Soon our notion of part-timers will encapsulate a wider group: those who do not want to take part in the daily nine-to-five rat race, or who want a greater degree of freedom and independence. There will still be a strong demand for the traditional, less than twenty hours a week, part-time work, but this will most likely be for a less skilled *doer* rather than a skilled consultant.

In a seller's market, employers will have to listen to employees' demands, among which a desire for greater freedom is likely to be prominent. Workers will want to be *asked* to achieve certain objectives, not *told* what to do. They are also likely to demand the chance to participate, to be involved in the company's goals at different levels.

FI Group and changing working practices

I have always worked in the computer software industry, which suffers from chronic skill shortages. When I was at ICL I realised that we were losing many workers who wanted a change in their working conditions. We would train analysts and programmers, some men and a lot of women, only to see them move on after five years or so, usually just as they were reaching their peak performance. These workers did not go to our competitors who were probably losing more people than we were. Many of the women employees simply decided they would like to have children; they decided that there were better alternatives than commuting to work every day. A number of those who dropped out later rejoined ICL but the vast majority felt they could have an improved quality of life by staying close to home, even if they had to take a menial part-time job locally and give up their IT career.

In the 1960s when I started the FI Group, computer link-ups were just becoming available. If we could connect these skilled computer professionals' homes via networks, we could offer them a chance to escape the rat race. Most of our work is task-oriented; it usually does not matter exactly when a job is finished, as long as it is completed before an agreed time. Once a terminal was installed in an analyst's or programmer's home, he or she had complete discretion over how and when they worked. Central computers never sleep. It did not matter whether our computer professionals worked from ten to four (am or pm), or in dribs and drabs throughout the day.

This opportunity to exercise control improved the quality of their lives and was just what these skilled professionals were looking for. It also meant that the FI Group could offer clients a service that was incomparably flexible and rapid. After all, our *offices* were open around the clock. This structure enabled us to tap into a skilled workforce that would otherwise have been unavailable: our technicians had on average twice the experience of those working for the competition.

Understandably, the competition were a little upset – not only because we had a competitive advantage, but also because they had trained our workers. Our current staff of about 1,000 have, on average, ten to fifteen years experience, which is a significant achievement for a relatively young industry.

The original concept of the FI Group has now been further expanded. Originally people worked only from their homes. Today, we can also set up a temporary office either in the client's building or in premises nearby. These offices are sited to be convenient for our employees. Our professional teams can call for help on other experts within the company from any part of the country. Such *neighbourhood work centres* are an extension of the idea of home working; they never develop the internal structures normally associated with offices, they are open round the clock and maintain the home feel.

Beyond flexitime

At the FI Group we feel we go beyond the idea of flexitime. In fact, flexitime is rather restrictive, as it does not give employees any real freedom in the way they choose to work. Our employees in contrast have a portfolio of jobs, rather than a simple choice of the hours they work. Our employees will not necessarily have more than one paid job, but they can commit themselves to other things besides the company. This freedom improves the quality of their lives. A golf fanatic, for instance, can play a round before starting work; a socialite can do a morning's work, have friends over for lunch, and then work from late afternoon to evening before having a night out; parents (and increasingly this applies to men as well as women) can structure their work day around school hours and time spent with their children.

In contrast to flexitime, this system gives people real freedom, and because most jobs are task oriented it has not hurt the performance of the FI Group. In fact, it improves company performance, because employees are happier and less stressed. Our work system improves the quality of our employees' lives and, in turn, they are more committed to the project in hand. Many more organizations will adopt this type of work structure in the next decade.

These new part-timers, with their portfolios of jobs, will force us also to reassess the benefits we offer non-full-time staff. For many years part-timers have been treated as second class, because there were always more workers than jobs and part-timers in particular were treated as fungible commodities. The new part-timers, however, will not consist simply of *doers*. Instead, they will be highly skilled consultants who will expect the same treatment as their conventional *full-time* equivalents. They will demand to be incorporated into the company pension scheme, and given full training and other corporate benefits. In turn, they will contribute the same loyalty and commitment to the firm as their full-time equivalents; indeed, because of their superior quality of life, their performance should meet a higher standard. (For a discussion of the effects of similar employee benefits in the John Lewis Partnership, see chapter 14.)

The crucial element is a commitment to training, because it is the incorporation of new ideas that drives a company forward. There must also be a commitment to new systems and technologies, which provide the added value that customers will expect. That, in turn, will be the key to a firm's competitive advantage in the 1990s.

7

Mentoring and the Development of Social Capital

Richard Caruso

Introduction

An organization's *expert* employees can be regarded as its *social capital*. Expert employees are distinguished by their skill or knowledge; their talents represent an essential part of an organization's strategic plan and are essential for its competitiveness. They may hold various types of positions, including management, technical and *know-how* jobs. Collectively these knowledge employees we refer to as a firm's *social capital*.

Both macro and micro economic factors are forcing organizations to think harder about their social capital. Just as businesses now develop strategic plans for their finance capital, some organizations may be obliged to plan similar strategies for their social capital. Indeed, in certain instances social capital may be more important than finance capital. In chapter 15 I develop the concept of social capital and lay the foundations for a new management strategy which likens it to finance capital.

Given the heightened importance of social capital, managers need to find new ways to attract, develop and retain key employees (see chapter 12). The practice of mentoring – by which an experienced individual guides someone who is less experienced – is becoming an increasingly important element in an organization's social capital strategy.[1]

Macro and micro economic trends and social capital

Labour and product market trends suggest that expert employees are becoming scarce and increasingly important to business organizations (see chapter 3).[2] Competition renders it increasingly important for managers to optimise the use of human resources. In addition, microeconomic factors – specifically, the raised expectations of strategically located, skilled individuals – are forcing certain businesses to reappraise their human capital strategies. The combination of these factors is moving social capital to the centre stage of management strategies to gain sustained competitive advantage.

Traditionally in most Western organizations employment relations have been resolved either through collective bargaining or through a firm's personnel functions. Collective bargaining and personnel functions deal largely with employee social welfare problems, and operate by reacting to problems. Generally they do not generate new ideas. In resolving problems they characteristically emphasise a collective or equalising approach. However, long term trends in labour and product markets, and changes in technology and legislation, are shifting the emphasis from *collective* to *individual* bargaining (Beer *et al.*, 1984).

Over the past twenty-five years demographic changes in labour supply have been dramatic. Labour is becoming increasingly scarce and heterogeneous. Further, changes in labour demand suggest that the largest growth areas will be services, where historically labour has not been strong collectively. Changes in technology also suggest that employers in some sectors are intensifying their search for more flexible and skilled employees. Finally, legislation, especially in Britain, has eroded support for collective bargaining by providing employees with individual rights. Together these trends suggest that specific employers will need to reappraise the status of their social capital.

Theories of career development have concentrated upon individuals within organizations suggesting that people develop careers by moving upward through a hierarchy. Success is equated with organizational position, without regard to individual personal development. Position, however, may have little relation to competence. Indeed, in a typical pyramid organization there may not be enough positions in the upper echelons to accommodate all those with the ability to occupy them. Further, political and bureaucratic dimensions of organizations sometimes inhibit individual personal development.

In this situation an individual has two options: (i) leave, or (ii) find ways around structures which prevent individual growth. A considerable deterrent to the first option, assuming demand is high for the individual's skills, is that another organization might prove to be equally bureaucratic and unconducive to individual growth. Accordingly, individuals might prefer to remain with their current employer and either accept the *status quo* or attempt to enhance their careers, and their personal development, by other means.

To this end, some individuals seek out mentoring in their organizations. To the extent that mentoring fulfils the employee's personal ambitions, he or she may take a more favourable view of the organization and thereby become more productive. Neither collective bargaining nor traditional personnel functions adequately address these issues (Dalton and Thompson, 1986).

Organizationally planned mentoring

Motorola, the third largest electronics company in the United States, has one of the longest established *planned* mentoring programmes in the world. These are located in its two southern Florida facilities. Motorola introduced mentoring specifically to develop young engineering graduates into a cadre of leading-edge employees which are expected to contribute significantly to the company's future success.

Previous research has characterised such planned mentoring programmes as operated by Motorola as a one-to-one relationship between an experienced and a less experienced person: mentor and protege, respectively. Such relationships have been shown to be *driven* by ambitious proteges, with career development viewed as one of their most important outcomes (Levinson *et al.*, 1978; Lea, 1981; Phillips-Jones, 1982).

Empirical research on mentoring is misleading because of the way it has been structured. Although theoretical analysis suggests the potential for a broader definition of the mentor (Levinson *et al.*, 1978, p. 100), previous research has asked its subjects (proteges) to focus upon *one* person as a mentor, while responding to specific questions concerning mentoring activity. This approach: (i) restricts the source of potential mentoring activity, and (ii) reinforces the concept of mentoring as a *closed* system between two individuals. The failure of empirical research to consider the possibility that proteges derive developmental assistance from someone, or some institution, other than a single designated individual *mentor* (Alleman, 1982; Bottoms, 1981; Clawson, 1979), can add substantially to the costs of mentoring programmes without maximising their benefits.

Thus, the conventional approach to mentoring is flawed. Let us explain. Suppose a protege identifies and cultivates an experienced, senior person in the same organization who is willing and able to guide that protege's career. To the extent that both mentor and protege are satisfied, a *closed* mentoring relationship is established. But in an organizational setting, such as exists in Motorola, closed systems are threatened in at least three ways: (i) by the protege, (ii) by the mentor, and (iii) by the environment in which such relationships take place.

Proteges are either new to a specific job or relatively inexperienced recent entrants to an organization. (It is precisely because of their inexperience that they require mentoring.) Given that careers are often accelerated by political know-how as well as technical knowledge, the protege would do best to choose a mentor from a senior cadre of managers, outside his or her functional line of command. However, proteges' knowledge of an organization and its senior managers is necessarily limited at the point when they wish to choose mentors.

Thus, potential organizational mentors may not respond positively to an approach from a protege. Indeed, senior and experienced individuals within an organization may: (i) perceive that they do not have time to devote to mentoring activities, (ii) not be motivated to engage in such relationships, since the organization does not reward them for doing so, (iii) be more committed to their own careers than to the organization and its employees, (iv) fear that sponsoring a protege would incur some form of social disapprobation, and (v) not have the knowledge and experience to help. For these reasons, proteges may not view a closed system mentoring relationship as the best way to enhance their career development. Instead, they may look for other types of help available within the organization.

Given the imperfect information available to proteges, those who do identify an individual mentor may well choose someone who is not entirely appropriate, who may be unable or unwilling to offer them satisfactory assistance. Under such circumstances, these proteges too may seek alternative forms of career development help. These processes militate against closed mentoring relationships.[3]

A further problem with closed mentoring relationships is that they work well only when mentor and protege can meet freely and regularly. The more structured the organization, the more difficult it is to maintain such a relationship. In effect, bureaucracy – a fact of life in most relatively large organizations – creates an environment hostile to closed mentoring systems, rendering them less effective and encouraging proteges to seek alternative ways to further their own career development.

In an organizational setting, the traditional conception of closed mentoring relationships is not entirely realistic. It might be more appropriate to view mentoring as an *open* rather than a closed activity. In an open system, a protege looks to a variety of sources for help in career development, rather than just one individual. An open system of mentoring might include sources of help outside the organization (eg, professional organizations, formal education, self-help, family and friends), as well as multiple sources within the organization (eg, individuals other than a formal mentor, training programmes, networking, specific job assignments and organizational culture).[4]

Motorola study

To investigate further the nature of mentoring activity the Business Performance Group carried out a study of the mentoring programmes in Motorola's two southern Florida facilities. By using data from interviews and from questionnaire surveys of both proteges and mentors, we established that mentoring activity is *open* rather than *closed*. Our findings suggest that if companies implement and operate mentoring programmes on the basis that the activity is *open*, they stand a much better chance of successfully husbanding and developing their human resources.

We chose Motorola for three reasons. First, its two southern Florida facilities operate one of the longest established planned mentoring programmes in the world. Second, the programme is adequately resourced and follows the generally accepted principles of best practice. Third, Motorola's programme has a traditional *closed* mentoring system. We believe that these are circumstances very much weighted against *open* mentoring. We felt that if we could establish the existence of protege driven open mentoring under these conditions, with a company of the stature of Motorola, it is reasonable to assume that open mentoring is a significant phenomenon which managers need to take into account in their human resource planning.

To test our hypothesis of open mentoring, we needed to depart from the flawed methodology of prior mentoring research which currently influences management practice. This traditional approach typically required a protege to identify a single individual as a mentor and then answer a series of questions pertaining to his or her relationship with that person. Such research has not considered the possibility that a protege might receive mentoring help from a variety of sources, and further, has neglected to consider the possible role of company culture in mentoring relationships.[5]

In 1980 mentoring at Motorola was given high visibility, supported by both the corporate leadership and the communications sector's management, in particular by George Fisher, then the general manager of the Boynton Beach paging facility. Fisher is credited with having started planned mentoring in the company's southern Florida sector. In 1984, when Fisher was promoted and transferred to Motorola's Illinois headquarters, the mentoring programme in southern Florida appeared to lose an important supporter. In January 1988, Fisher became president and CEO of Motorola worldwide.

Fisher's replacement in the communications sector was reportedly more oriented toward short term results. Accordingly, the human resource and personnel functions were given less resources than requested. As of 1984, moreover, the huma . resource function was asked to report to site personnel in Florida, as opposed to corporate management. According to a participant in the mentoring programme, the corporate human resource function is, 'effective and interested in [mentoring] as change agents but less interested in it as a continuing programme.' It has 'a mission of identifying the stars of the new group and facilitating their career development.' However, members of the sector personnel department, which administered the programme from 1985, perceived their role 'as attempting to treat everybody equally regardless of their ability or potential'.

It seems that initially, the mentoring programme received corporate support, was relatively well resourced financially and employed senior communications sector managers. Over the years, however, the programme lost the apparent support of sector managers who were transferred. As a result, the programme became less visible. Nonetheless, we were assured that proteges were adequately trained and introduced to the concepts of mentoring. This was confirmed by our observation and interview data. Further the programme itself for actual participants appeared to be adequately administered.

Findings

Table 7.1 reports mean ratings of help received by proteges in each of three help categories: specific learning, general career development and personal help from the assigned mentor and five alternative potential sources of mentoring help.

All means are derived from a five-point Likert scale (1 = None and 5 = Great) and indicate the amount of help proteges receive from each source. Standard deviations are shown in parentheses; in italics are *t* statistics for differences between the means for the assigned mentor and the specific alternative source. Thus, the *12.74 t* statistic reported in the 'Specific Learning' column and the 'Self-Help' row represents the difference between the mean ratings for specific learning assistance received from the assigned mentor (1.91) and from self-help (3.14).

Data strongly support our dispersal hypothesis. Indeed, proteges in Motorola obtain significantly more mentoring help from sources outside the company's formal programme than they do from their assigned mentor.

Specific learning

Data reported in the first column of Table 7.1 refers to the specific learning proteges receive from the assigned mentor and unofficial sources of help. In keeping with the predictions of our theory proteges

Table 7.1 The dispersal and nature of mentoring help obtained by proteges

Categories of Mentoring Help

Source of Mentoring Help	Specific Learning Mean (std dev) *t*	General Career Development Mean (std dev) *t*	Personal Help Mean (std dev) *t*
Assigned Mentor	1.91 (0.86)	1.98 (0.92)	2.01 (1.03)
Supervisor	3.19 (0.99) *11.95**	3.09 (1.02) *9.18**	2.81 (0.99) *6.35**
Self-Help	3.14 (1.07) *12.74**	2.71 (1.12) *6.55**	2.31 (1.18) *1.99*
Rest of Org.	3.10 (0.79) *11.36**	2.64 (0.79) *6.21**	2.49 (0.90) *4.14**
Outside Rels.	2.00 (1.03) *0.63*	2.15 (1.01) *1.46*	2.55 (1.17) *4.08**
Prof. Bodies	1.73 (1.11) *1.73*	1.72 (1.03) *2.51**	1.43 (0.90) *5.65**

[n = 134]

t statistic between mean of category and mean of assigned mentor

* significant at or above the 99 percent level

perceive that they receive a relatively small amount of help in this regard from assigned mentors. This contrasts sharply with the assistance they receive from unofficial mentoring sources. Immediate supervisors were most helpful, closely followed by self-help and assistance from other sources within the organization. That proteges receive significantly more specific learning help from supervisors is not surprising since assigned mentors are often deliberately drawn from areas of the company less accessible to proteges. More striking is the significant amount of informal mentoring proteges obtain from the rest of the organization and from self-help.

General career development

A similar pattern is observed for general career development. Proteges receive significantly more help of this kind from supervisors, self-help and other organizational sources than they do from their assigned mentors. The differences between the relevant means are all highly significant, at or above the 99 percent level (see Table 7.1). Professional organizations are the least helpful with regard to general career development. Since proteges are young, recent recruits, they are presumably at a point in their careers when they do not rely too heavily on professional organizations. Nor is it surprising that outside relationships are more helpful with career development than with learning specific work tasks.

Personal help

As might be expected, proteges receive significantly more help with regard to personal help from their outside relationships than from the official company mentor. The only potential source of personal help which proteges rate less helpful than their assigned mentors is *professional bodies*. The other four alternative sources are significantly more important to proteges than their assigned mentor: t statistics are significant at or above the 99 percent level.

Conclusion

Mentoring research has focused on one-to-one relationships between two individuals, a protege and a mentor. There has been little recognition that mentoring might take some other form. In particular, mentoring has not been examined empirically as a protege driven dispersed social activity and this can be a considerable cost to company's human resource stratgies.

Our research at Motorola, reported here, determined that the formally assigned mentor, although heavily resourced, was not the protege's primary source of mentoring help. Equally important is the fact that no single individual supplied most of the help received by the proteges: in other words, proteges did not simply substitute a naturally selected mentor for the one designated by the company. Results suggest that exclusive one-to-one mentoring relationships are rare and cannot be successfully legislated by a business organization.

The use of planned mentoring programmes by business organizations is still relatively new, but increasingly popular. Our research yielded some important insights into how Motorola's planned mentoring programme actually works, and the role a planned mentoring programme might actually play in a business organization.

More specifically, the empirical data from our questionnaire survey strongly supports our view of mentoring as a protege driven open system. Proteges seek and receive needed mentoring help from a number of sources, many of which Motorola makes available. This bottom-up dispersed activity departs from the traditional view of mentoring as a one-to-one activity between two individuals. It also contrasts with the idea that one-to-one mentors drive the relationship from the top-down. While conducting our empirical test on site at Motorola, we observed that experienced managers who have the capacity to be one-to-one mentors are kept very busy satisfying a multitude of demands, and frequently do not have the time to function as a one-to-one mentor for a protege.

Our study also demonstrated that: (i) proteges recognize a need for mentoring help, (ii) make an effort to obtain such help and (iii) obtain much of the help they need from a variety of sources, mostly within Motorola. We also found that assigned mentors and proteges take different views of the nature of their formal relationship. The proteges believe the assigned mentors provide much less help than the mentors believe they provide. Mentors believe proteges make less effort to obtain help than proteges believe they make.

Proteges also believe that a principal role of the assigned mentor is to serve as a *safety net*. Although mentors were not the proteges' primary source of mentoring help, our data suggest that proteges nonetheless obtained much of the mentoring help they needed. Proteges and mentors both indicated that mentoring influences and is reflective of Motorola's culture. However, we do not have sufficient data to suggest more precise interrelationships between mentoring, Motorola's culture and the role of the mentoring programme.

Although we discovered that the mentoring programme was not working the way Motorola told participants it would, proteges nonetheless obtained many of the mentoring benefits that Motorola intended the programme to provide, mostly from organizational sources. We do not, however, have sufficient data to determine whether this outcome results from participation in the programme, or is independent of such participation. Our data do not permit us to determine the extent to which the mentoring programme itself facilitated or hindered naturally occurring mentoring processes at Motorola.

In implementing its mentoring programme, Motorola followed the principles of best practice, trained programme participants in traditional one-to-one mentoring theory, and dedicated significant resources to the programme. In many respects, then, these are circumstances under which it should have been unusually difficult to view mentoring as something other than the traditional one-to-one relationship. Yet our empirical results strongly support the hypothesis that proteges seek and receive help from a variety of sources. Thus, there seems to be potential for a wider application of our view of mentoring as a protege driven open system.

Applicability of this research to practice

Recently, the author was asked by the director of training at Motorola's communications sector in southern Florida to present the results of this study to the sector engineering management personnel, and also to the sector coordinator of the mentoring programme. The study results were accepted as helpful by both engineering management and the mentoring programme coordinator. The mentoring programme coordinator asked the author to suggest ways in which the programme might be changed to reflect what was learned in this study.

In this spirit, three major suggestions were made and recently adopted by Motorola. First, initial training for both proteges and mentors should indicate that mentoring need not be a one-to-one direct relationship, but might involve multiple sources of help sought by the protege; many of these sources are made available by Motorola. Training should also point out that a primary goal of the programme is to facilitate proteges' socialization into Motorola, and that the assigned mentor is not only a potential direct source of help but functions as a *safety net* when other sources fail. Second, assigned mentors should be advised that they may need to kickstart a protege mentoring relationship, yet they should not necessarily view themselves as the focal point of protege mentoring activity. Finally, we recommended a periodic objective evaluation of the programme, to identify any problems and to obtain a fuller understanding of mentoring activity. We also suggested that further research be undertaken to examine the interrelationship between open system mentoring at Motorola and the corporate culture.

Since these suggestions have only recently been adopted, we have not been able to determine their effect, if any, on mentoring at Motorola. That must remain a topic for further research.

8

Management Development and Career Success

David Guest, Riccardo Peccei and Patrice Rosenthal

Explaining the problem of management development

The importance of management development is widely acknowledged. Indeed it was rated the top human resource management priority in one recent United Kingdom survey of senior executives. At the same time many analysts refer to the *problem* of management development. Comparing Britain's practice with that of key competitor countries, the Handy Report (Handy, 1987) characterised management development as 'too little, too late and for too few'. Much anguished debate ensued, but apart from a limited number of company developments, the main response has been a mushrooming of MBA programmes.

If management development is so important, why has there been so little activity? It is important to address this question before we call for more management development. Otherwise our exhortations may fall on deaf ears, as top managers continue to pay lip service to the concept without carrying through to action. This chapter suggests a possible explanation and reports on a preliminary test.

Management development comprises a range of activities, from formal training courses to informal learning processes closely tied to the job, such as coaching and shadowing (Mumford, 1989). In practice, however, management development is often equated with training courses to the exclusion of more informal activities (Storey, 1989). Our major hypothesis is that little management development takes place because there is insufficient evidence that it does any good. This in turn reflects the problems of evaluating management development and the general lack of enthusiasm for the serious evaluation of any kind of personnel activity.

As Davies (1983) argues, a systematic evaluation of management training-development requires an analysis on several levels: reaction, learning, individual job performance, and organizational performance. It is relatively easy to evaluate participating managers' reactions to a development programme and to assess what they learned. The future orientation of management development activities makes it difficult to extend an evaluation beyond those levels, however. Problems include the definition of appropriate, clearly measurable criteria for success, and the need to control for other influences on individual or organizational performance.

Indeed it appears that little effort is made to evaluate management development efforts. Saari *et al.* (1988) in a United States survey, found that 50 per cent of management development was not evaluated; where evaluation did take place, it typically consisted of end of course forms, which tend to be of more value to the trainer than the trainee. Similarly the Cranfield-Price Waterhouse survey of European human resource management (Syrett, 1990) found that although managers claimed to do some sort of evaluation, they typically could not provide detailed information on what they did. Mumford's (1988) study of 41 United Kingdom based organizations concluded there was almost no evaluation of management development.

In this vacuum, there is considerable scope for individual managers to reach their own conclusions as to the impact and usefulness of management development activities. Their interpretations may reflect organizational values and traditions, personal values or personal experience. In short, evaluation becomes a political process (Hesseling, 1966).

An organization's management development strategy will be shaped by the beliefs of its top managers. The implementation of policy will be shaped by managers at various levels who must decide whether to sponsor subordinates (or indeed apply themselves) to participate in formal management development activities, or to initiate informal development processes. It is therefore crucial to understand the beliefs of these decision makers and of potential participants in management development. In particular, because plant managers' influence on the development of other managers in the plant may increase as organizations become more decentralised, their beliefs become critical.

We also need to know something about the source of these beliefs, which might include:

1 *The shared values derived from a strong organizational culture.* Some organizations have a reputation for supporting management development, while others prefer to meet their requirements on the

labour market. Some writers have emphasised that a supportive organizational culture is important for management development.

2	*The presumed link between business and corporate strategy and management development.* An extensive literature has emphasised the need to integrate management development with corporate strategy (eg, Tichy *et al* 1982). However, this integration will not necessarily result in more management development. One approach to human resource strategy focuses on making full use of employees' capabilities, a goal to which training and development contribute. Another school, however, sees human resource management primarily as a matter of increasing efficiency through more flexible organization of work and use of employees. Armstrong (1989) has claimed that this is the dominant approach in the United Kingdom, reflecting in turn the dominance of accountants and their short term systems of financial control. From an accounting perspective, the main question is whether the benefits of management development exceed its costs. (See chapter 10 for some dilemmas facing management accountants.) As discussed above, however, the nature of management development makes it virtually impossible to assemble firm evidence on this point.

3	*Personal experience.* Those who feel they have benefited from management development themselves may be more likely to support it for others (and *vice versa*). We know from the Handy Report that 75 per cent of top managers in the United Kingdom did not go to university. They may feel that if they succeeded through a Darwinian process of the survival of the fittest, then that approach is good enough for others (for an alternative discussion of this point, see chapter 5). By implication, management development is for *softies*.

This analysis views judgements about management development as a subjective political process – as must be the case, given the uncertainty and unpredictability arising from the inadequacies of formal evaluation. In *strong* organizational cultures, to use Schein's (1985) term, the culture will shape beliefs about the importance of management development and the forms it should take. In *weaker* cultures, beliefs will be influenced mainly by individual experiences. Whether the organizational culture is strong or weak, more research on beliefs about the efficacy of management development is needed before we can understand policy and practice in this complex field.

Management development can contribute to both organizational and individual success; individuals are likely to have views on both effects.

Given the tenuous links between management development and organizational success, their views about its contribution to individual career success are likely to be more firmly held. For many managers, this will be a key criterion in considering management development for themselves: ('will it help me to advance my career?').

Management development can contribute to career success in at least four ways. First, attendance on management development programmes may be a formalised criterion for career advancement. Sometimes, for example, a group of managers is designated as *high potential*, with both development programmes and career progression following as a consequence. In other organizations completion of certain training courses may be a condition for advancement. The second route is a political or instrumental one. Attendance on development courses may give managers access to influential contacts and networks conducive to advancement of their career. Third, management development can help managers acquire particular skills and expertise that are considered necessary for advancement. And finally, management development may lead to an improvement in performance in the current job, and in turn to promotion. As organizations move towards a greater emphasis on *performance*, this fourth route may play a larger part in individuals' views of management development. It also has the value of appearing more relevant and immediately beneficial.

Research on the causes of career success

Mangham and Silver (1986) show that in any given year many companies provide no training, and many managers receive no training and development other than measures they initiate. Indeed the idea that individuals should take initiatives for themselves remains popular, and many of those currently studying for conventional MBAs are not sponsored by their companies. Edwards (1987) found that only one in six factory managers had any experience of formal management development. However, those who had spent some time working in their company's head office appeared to have rather different attitudes, and in particular to give greater weight to *people issues*. Apparently certain types of work experience provide important development opportunities.

Mumford (1988) surveyed 144 directors and found that few had received formal training and management development, few recognised any organizational plans for their careers and almost none attributed their success to formal development experiences. While 'the vast majority of directors identified job experiences and particular job contents as being crucial in their development, these were generally seen as unaffected by formal management development processes', (Mumford, 1988, p. 17). Attitudes to most training courses were described as 'rather grey in tone', reflecting the directors' perception that they lacked relevance and application. In some cases, Mumford notes, centrally planned management development declines as organizations divisionalise and decentralise.

Despite the controversy aroused by the Handy report, Keep (1989) suggests, its publication has led to little real change. He reports extensive discussion of Handy's suggestions and considerable publicity for developments in certain companies. However, these companies are relatively few in number and are typically competing in well defined international markets where improvements in human resource utilisation are essential to their survival.

Management development is usefully placed in context by studies that explore the criteria by which chief executives explain their career success and development. Margerison (1980) and Margerison and Kakabadse (1985) report that United Kingdom and United States chief executives consider personal factors to be the key influences on their career development. Specifically, a need to achieve results, an ability to work with a range of people, challenge and a willingness to take risks come top of the list. Only then do forms of experience come into play; these include early responsibility and a wide range of early experiences. Dakin and Hamilton (1985) find that managers in New Zealand believe that certain types of on the job experience were the key to their success.

Storey (1990), perhaps optimistically summarising this research, reports that senior managers in various countries 'are drawn from a wide range of social backgrounds and, in the main, attribute their capabilities to a wide range of hands-on experience' (Storey, 1990, p. 7). However, Kotter (1982) denies the relevance of specific types of experience for later success, at least in general management. He also claims that almost all types of management courses have little bearing on subsequent success. What matters instead is a complex growth in a range of relevant knowledge and skills.

Together these studies show a widespread belief among managers that personal characteristics are the foremost determinants of career success, and that their practical experience is crucial. But this experience is usually not described as planned development, and conventional management development programmes do not figure prominently. Advocates of management development may well be disturbed by such findings.

Let us hypothesise that, given the difficulty of evaluating management development, beliefs about the value of management development are shaped either by a strong organizational culture or by personal experience, and that chief executives play a key role in shaping culture,

(Schein, 1985). Many United Kingdom executives have not been to university, most have not had extensive formal management development and most explain their career progress in terms of personal factors rather than management development. They are therefore unlikely to shape a culture which emphasises management development. At best, they will pay lip service to the idea, but devolve responsibility for implementation to the personnel/management development function (see chapter 5 for an opposing view to this thesis among the largest 50 United Kingdom companies).

The managers in question can then be expected to formalise and bureaucratise management development as a means of ensuring control (Guest, 1990). The resulting formal systems will receive general support but will typically be seen as slightly detached from the mainstream of key organizational activity. Management development will be defined in terms of courses, which will be perceived as *a good thing*, but not the key to organizational and career success. Once such formal activities and beliefs have become established, even sophisticated management developers will find it difficult to change the system.

Research framework

We wanted to test the hypotheses outlined above by exploring perceptions within organizations, comparing different types of managers (in particular those with more and less successful careers) to see whether the perceptions reported for chief executives and directors are widely shared. At the same time we wanted to develop and test a conceptual framework which would help us understand these perceptions and their policy implications.

Our conceptual framework begins with the assumption that formal evaluation of management development, based on conventional evaluation frameworks, (eg, Hamblin, 1974; Davies, 1983), has limited value because of the severe problems of controlling for other changes and interpreting observations. Therefore influential evaluations will almost inevitably be informal and subjective. Sometimes they will centre on judgements about how management development contributes to organizational success. For certain types of management development (eg, those designed to change the organizational culture and therefore administered to large numbers of managers indiscriminately), some criteria of organizational performance may well be appropriate. However, most management development is directed towards individuals, typically those of high potential. In such cases certain organizational criteria may still be appropriate (eg, the availability of candidates of high potential in succession plans), but some measure of contribution to individual managers' careers is likely to be more important.

The second major element of our conceptual framework is the application of attribution theory to explanations of career success. Attribution theory (Hewstone, 1988; Weiner *et al.*, 1971) proposes that individuals actively seek to make sense of the world around them – for example, by interpreting events in the light of their supposed causes. Achievement related behaviour is a case in point. Attribution theory proposes that one's understanding of and reactions to success or failure are based largely on the perceived causes of that success or failure.

At its simplest level, attribution theory identifies two different types of explanation or cause: those that are internal to the person and those that are located in the environment. Certain attributional patterns or tendencies can also be identified. For example, people tend to believe that they are personally (internally) responsible for their successes, but that their failures are the result of external factors. Those for whom achievement is particularly important are more likely to assume that both success and failure result from internal causes.

This line of reasoning suggests that senior managers would be likely to explain their own career success, and probably the success or failure of others, in terms of internal factors such as ability and need for achievement, rather than external factors such as management development programmes. Adopting a *survival of the fittest* model, they may therefore believe that the best managers will rise to the top on the basis of their own drive and ability. The less able may require some form of help, including management development, but it is not likely to be greatly valued by aspiring high fliers. Earlier surveys confirm that chief executives and directors attach considerable importance to internal personal factors when they think about the causes of successful careers.

Research study

We have been exploring these issues empirically by conducting interviews with managers – some highly successful, some less successful – at various stages of their careers, to learn more about their attitudes to management development. One reason for extending the sample beyond chief executives and directors is that responsibility for management development is increasingly devolved. Furthermore if formal and informal management development are to be integrated, much of the responsibility for implementation will rest with managers below policy making level. Managers at various levels within an organization will be deciding whether to take up development activities for themselves and/ or their staff. Accordingly, our sample includes not only those who will formulate policy for management development, but those who will implement that policy and participate in development programmes.

The survey covers various aspects of management development, learning, and careers, and makes explicit use of attribution theory. In particular it examines perceptions of the four ways (outlined earlier) in which management development may influence career success. The research is being conducted in organizations in different sectors, but all with a strong professional component among the management staff. Such environments are of interest to us because of the strong tradition of formal education associated with the professions as well as organizations' growing need to emphasise managerial skills and expertise.

In this chapter we present some preliminary descriptive findings from the first of our organizations. The results reported here are restricted to the question of whether managers perceive a link between management development and career success, without regard to how that link is created.

The sample consisted of forty-nine managers – twenty-nine clinical staff and twenty non-clinical – in a district of the National Health Service which has been preparing its case for Trust status.[1] In terms of organizational status, they ranged from the unit general manager to senior supervisors. These managers were likely to have given some thought to management development, since one of the criteria for Trust status is the quality of human resource management. It should be noted that this National Health Service unit is in a state of considerable turbulence and uncertainty – a circumstance that may have some bearing on the perceived role of management development.

1) Importance of management development. Responses to our survey indicate that management development is highly valued in the organization. Fully 86 per cent agree that 'attendance on formal management development programmes is essential for someone who wants to make career progress in the National Health Service'. More personally, 57 per cent agree that 'formal management development activities in the National Health Service are extremely valuable for career development'. In practice management development appears to be defined largely in terms of off the job courses.

2) Determinants of career success. Respondents were asked what should, and what does, determine career success in this section of the National Health Service? The forty-nine managers gave a total of 120 responses to the first question, and 122 responses to the second. The results are summarised in table 8.1.

Training and development is not accorded a high priority. It ranks fourth among the factors that should, and almost last among the factors that in practice do, determine career success. Knowledge, skills, and expertise (both managerial and professional/technical) are considered to be important, but this result says nothing about how

Table 8.1 Determinants of career success

	Should determine	Actually determine
Ability	14	11
Motivation	6	4
Knowledge, skills, expertise	26	17
Training and development	14	4
Qualifications	4	6
Experience	10	11
Achievements/past performance	15	7
Commitment	8	3
Personal qualities	17	17
Administrative convenience	0	15
Political factors	6	27
Total	120	122

these skills are acquired. The research cited earlier suggests that managers might say they acquired their knowledge through experience, while professionals would additionally give some emphasis to initial education and professional training. In practice many of our respondents believed that political factors and administrative convenience, reflective perhaps of a bureaucratic environment, were critical influences on career success.

The data in table 8.1 may reflect stereotypes about how the organization works, but it should be remembered that the respondents include those who have to make it work. Although considerable lip service is paid to management development, it is not seen as a primary means of career progress. Its influence, if any, operates through the third and fourth of the routes outlined earlier; that is, management development *qualifies* managers for promotion by helping them to acquire knowledge, skills, and expertise or to improve their current performance.

3) Management development and personal careers. Respondents were also asked about the factors determining their own career progress. A large majority (88 per cent) were satisfied, and only 8 per cent dissatisfied, with their careers to date. Their criteria of success varied significantly. Many were concerned with progress up the hierarchy or against some career plan, but others emphasised the importance of job content and job satisfaction; some wanted to make a contribution to the National Health Service, and still others were concerned about the balance between home and work.

Thirty-seven of the forty-nine respondents felt that their careers had been hindered in some way. The personal circumstance of being a married woman was mentioned thirteen times; lack of appropriate training, skills or experience was cited fourteen times. The other key factor mentioned was the lack of local opportunities either to progress or to invest in training and development. When asked to explain the constraints on their careers, that is, most people cited external circumstances beyond their control, including the lack of appropriate training and development. It is worth noting that most respondents had been on a number of short training courses, concerned mainly with business and interpersonal/management skills, in the last three years, and several had attended longer term development courses.

When respondents were asked about their own career progress compared with that of others who had joined the National Health Service at about the same time, most thought they themselves had done better. In explaining this relative performance, no one cited anything to do with education, training or development. As a slightly different approach, respondents were asked to think of others who had done better and worse than they had in their careers, and to identify the explanatory factors. The main factors cited had to do with motivation, career drive and ability. Knowledge was mentioned twice and skills six times in explaining why a colleague was more successful; they were cited once and three times respectively in relation to less successful colleagues. In short, training and career development are not seen as critical factors differentiating the more and less successful in their careers.

Policy implications

The results presented here may seem to reflect rather puzzling and contradictory views of management development. However, they are consistent with our conceptual framework.

Survey responses reveal attitudes and beliefs about management development at three levels. On the surface there is widespread agreement that participation in management development programmes is generally an important factor determining career progress (ie, management development is a good thing). At the second level, when considering National Health Service policy and practice, respondents characterise management development (both in itself and as reflected in knowledge, skills and qualifications) as something which is considerably less important in practice than it ought to be. At the third level, when respondents were asked what differentiated the more and less successful, management development almost disappeared from the lists.

Instead, responses were dominated by factors internal to individuals and consonant with the predictions from attribution theory.

Although the analysis is still in its preliminary stages, the results appear to support the hypotheses derived from attribution theory. Most managers pointed to internal factors when asked to explain their success compared with others. It is more difficult to examine lack of success since most respondents claimed to be successful. However, the citing of uncontrollable external factors, such as family circumstances or non-availability of training, as barriers to career progress is consonant with the theory. Again in line with the theory, managers tend to explain the career success and failure of others in terms of internal factors and to ignore influences such as management development.

These findings help to explain why lip service is paid to the importance of management development but in practice it is not seen as a critical influence on career success. Some sort of management development, or at least the possession of appropriate knowledge and skills, is regarded as helpful but not essential to success. Until perceptions alter, the prospects for a greater commitment to management development may not be encouraging.

The dramatic changes now being made in the National Health Service provide an opportunity to alter perceptions. However, the omens are not good. Sixty-eight per cent of respondents agreed that they need to take responsibility for their own career development since no one else will. Their priorities for personal training and development centre on acquisition of *hard* business skills, preferably through short courses. However, when asked about priorities for their immediate boss, they put interpersonal skills training at the top of the list. Personal priorities therefore differ from those perceived more widely in the organization.

The interest in short courses in business skills may reflect the changes now under way in the National Health Service. As the unit moves from a professional bureaucracy to a more business oriented organization, there is at least a belief that training and development should be able to help. Some of the professional medical and paramedical staff would like to attend courses to help them become more business-like. In contrast, some of the support managers are more interested in longer term professional development and acquisition of qualifications such as an MBA. In this they are perhaps reflecting the importance always attached to qualifications in a medical bureaucracy.

In the climate of change and ambiguity, training and development are seen as one way to master uncertainty. But development is still defined in terms of off the job courses. A policy-driven emphasis on the role of training and development could help to create more positive percep-tions for the future. Policy makers could seize this opportunity to translate the desire to learn into effective learning by promoting a range of learning processes. This will happen only if the policy makers first decide that they wish to give some real weight to the role of training and development, however.

This study also highlights the link between organizational culture and management development. It should be possible to classify management development cultures and identify the types of management development found in each. For example in a bureaucratic environment such as the National Health Service, management development is seen as a formal activity (attendance on courses). An important first step in analysing management development in organizations would be to diagnose the relevant dimensions of organizational culture by exploring beliefs about management development. This chapter has reported the first steps along this path.

ORGANIZATION AND HUMAN RESOURCES

9

People and Quality

Stephen Hill

Introduction

Top managers today need no convincing that the quality of their company's products, and of its production processes, is vital to its success, indeed its very survival. Japanese manufacturers put quality on the agenda of British and American business in the early 1980s, by demonstrating that customers preferred quality goods, and that delivering quality was largely a function of the competence of management. Certain principles of management, they showed, could be synthesised into a powerful business discipline that enabled companies to become more efficient by keeping costs down while improving product quality; to be more innovative in creating new market opportunities and devising new products and better ways of producing them; and to respond more rapidly and flexibly to change. In the last ten years, methods of managing for quality have been widely disseminated, and many companies now have several years' experience of using these approaches.

Modern quality management has two faces. The *hard* aspect is the pursuit of improved product quality by means of rigorous analytical techniques such as *statistical process control* and financial measures such as *the cost of quality*. The *soft* aspect is the mobilisation of a company's human resources behind the goal of continuous business improvement. Extensive training, more participation, decentralisation of decision-making, and new ways of treating employees are needed to win the active commitment of everyone in the firm. Thus quality management must be understood *both* as *managing for quality* and as *managing in a quality way*. In this second sense, it exemplifies the recent trend among Western businesses to seek cultural change within their organizations as a major component of their strategies for competitive success.

Members of the London School of Economics Business Performance Group have studied the implementation of quality management in Britain, from the early days of piecemeal reforms (such as quality circles) through to the holistic, company-wide implementation of total quality management, which aims to improve every aspect of a business. This chapter will discuss the theory and development of quality management, and report some of our findings.

Background

The two pioneers of quality control (QC) were American: W E Deming and J M Juran. But their ideas and techniques were taken up systematically and on a large scale in Japan rather than in the United States or Europe. In the late 1940s and early 1950s, the Japanese Union of Scientists and Engineers (JUSE) developed and popularised Deming's work on statistical methods for quality control, the first Quality Control Annual Conference was held in 1951, and from the outset JUSE targeted both engineers and foremen. Training programmes for foremen, known as 'workshop QC study groups', were a feature of the QC movement throughout the 1950s and were renamed 'QC circle' activities in 1962. Some estimate that several million foremen and other employees had been trained and were members of circles by the mid-1980s (Lillrank and Kano, 1989). Japanese companies were willing to commit significant resources to quality; the JUSE course for foremen lasts forty hours, for example.

Over time the Japanese shifted away from Deming's emphasis on statistical quality control for engineers and managers (which JUSE had extended to foremen) and began to regard QC as a tool of general management, with top managers as the prime movers. This shift reflected their assimilation of Juran's ideas. Ishikawa (1985) describes the change as a sequence that began with a view of quality control as inspection, moved to a broader concern with the manufacturing process and error prevention, and ended with total quality as a concern of the entire company, applied to every activity.

The evolution of the quality movement can also be seen as a change from focusing on manufacturing production, with a particular emphasis on engineering, to a general business discipline and culture. Some people now prefer the term 'continuous business improvement' as a more accurate description of the character and purpose of quality management.

By adding participation to QC, Japanese companies gave modern quality management its distinctive character. Participation means that quality management is informed by the widest possible knowledge, including that of the people directly involved in a task. In addition, involvement in the quality effort can benefit individual employees, by improving their motivation, morale, work environment and skills; in this sense participation promotes what Lillrank and Kano (1989, p. 15) call 'people building'.

Total quality management (TQM) is based on the premise that the quality of the final product or service is the result of every single activity carried out within an organization. Therefore every person and every process must be engaged in the quality effort. Each employee works to maintain and improve the quality of what he or she does, and works with others to enhance their collective activities. A successful outcome depends both on appropriate systems and on wide diffusion of an appropriate organizational culture of quality.

Principles of managing for quality

TQM has been described as 'a thought revolution in management' (Ishikawa, 1985, p. 1). In fact, the basic principles of managing to produce quality goods and services are simple and apply in all settings. The practical implementation of these principles is more difficult.

First, define quality

Quality in business means meeting customer requirements. The test is *fitness for use*, the extent to which a product or service successfully serves the purpose of the user. Fitness for use includes both 'quality of design' and 'quality of conformance' (Juran *et al.*, 1974). Design quality results from determining what fitness for use means to the customer: choosing a concept that meets the customer's needs and translating this into detailed specifications. Conformance quality means meeting these specifications.

Some people, focusing on conformance quality, have assumed that quality improvement just means controlling for defects, rather than first ensuring quality of design. But this approach fails to ask what the customer actually requires. If the product or service delivered is not exactly what the user wants, conformance to specification becomes irrelevant. Quality of conformance is a measure of *efficiency*, while quality of design is a measure of *effectiveness*. Put another way, first you need to know that you are doing the right thing; then you make sure that you are doing it right.

Second, define the customer

Among the American pioneers of quality control, fitness for use was at first identified with the needs of the final customer. Hence quality of design was to be determined by market research among potential customers, to ascertain their requirements. Ishikawa extended the idea to include *customers* within the organization. As each unit in an organization receives inputs from, and produces outputs for, other units, it is both a customer and a supplier of other units.

Now it is generally agreed that all transactions internal to the firm should be appraised for their quality of design. Managers need to ascertain the exact needs of those who use the output that they and their staff produce. Once requirements are determined, then managers can find the most efficient means of conforming to the specification. As a customer, each organization unit should expect conformance with its own requirements, while as a supplier it has an obligation to meet the requirements of its own *customers*.

Third, find appropriate standards of performance

In addition to market research among external and internal customers, some companies also use competitive benchmarking as a performance standard for the quality of design. They may analyse competitors' products or share information on processes among non-competitors, in order to establish performance targets based on the prevailing best practice. For example, a manufacturing company wishing to improve its stock control and order processing might set itself targets based on what a successful retailer has achieved.

Quality of conformance is measured by the amount of error-free production of goods and services, the aim being to get things right first time without defects or reworking. Quality of conformance has received the most attention historically, and a number of techniques to measure and control this aspect of quality are widely used.

Any organizational process which follows a structured and repetitive sequence of input-transformation-output can in principle be analysed by statistical techniques that measure variation with a view to identifying and acting on the causes of any variance (Oakland, 1989). In fact, statistical process control has a long history in manufacturing operations and is widely used today, even by companies which have not embarked on total quality. Outside manufacturing, however, the technique is difficult to apply, because of the problems in measuring performance and defining standards. The use of statistical techniques normally requires major changes in the sort of information companies collect and a systematic analysis of their processes.

The *cost of quality* is a financial measure of quality performance which allows companies to measure where they are in terms of design and conformance, to estimate the gains that would result from improvements, and to assess the cost effectiveness of their quality improvements. The costs of quality include: *failure costs*, which would disappear if a product or service could be produced with no defects; in effect, these are the costs of non-quality; *appraisal costs*, which are incurred when people have to check that things are right; these represent the costs of not being sure that non-quality has been eliminated; and *prevention costs*, which are incurred in the elimination of failure and appraisal costs, and represent the costs of the programme of quality improvement itself.

The *cost of quality* concept implies that quality improvement may need to stop short of some absolute standard of quality if further prevention costs would exceed the associated savings. There is a significant difference between Japanese and Western quality theorists on this issue. Ishikawa (1985), for example, regards QC as generally reducing costs while raising quality, and does not even consider the notion of a *cost of quality*. The American authorities, such as Crosby (1980) and Lundvall (1974), place considerable emphasis on such costs. This difference appears to reflect managerial cultures, with Western companies being dominated by notions of measurable payback and return on capital while the Japanese seem more willing to trust that quality benefits business and to proceed on faith.

The use of the *cost of quality* as a performance measure should lead to a real improvement in the collection and analysis of relevant information, and in setting priorities for improvement efforts. But its limitations should be clearly understood: all the components of the true cost cannot be measured. In particular, the costs of non-conformance may be calculated precisely while the costs of quality of design failures can only be guessed at. The crucial point that informs all quality improvement activity is that *what really costs money is not quality but non-quality*.

Fourth, top management must organize for quality

Top management is crucial to the success of quality improvement. All the theorists of quality management agree that managers at the highest level in a company must be committed to continuous quality improvement, understand the principles and be actively involved. The chief executive and fellow directors alone can set corporate quality policies and provide the resources. But they also have a leadership role, which means they should not settle for arm's length involvement. Practitioners of TQM recommend that training and implementation should start at the top and then cascade down through the organization.

The organizational arrangements normally include a steering committee comprising senior managers drawn from a wide range of functions and reporting directly to the top of the company. Its role is to oversee and allocate responsibility for the implementation of corporate quality policies. New arrangements also have to be made for organized communication between departments and across functions, because quality management requires greatly expanded flows of information and communication in order to identify and resolve issues. Most existing large organizations promote compartmentalism and an inward-looking attitude among members of organizational sub-units. The introduction of the *internal customer* principle helps to open up communication and improve co-ordination. But firms embarking on systematic quality management also feel the need for more formal arrangements, such as interdepartmental and cross-functional committees, and special project teams. Teamworking and other small group activities for quality improvement are introduced throughout the organization.

Fifth, quality is built on the participation of employees

Managing for quality involves a greater number of people in decision-making. New committees and quality improvement project teams will by themselves extend the numbers involved in decisions. Ishikawa (1985) firmly believes that the participation of all employees from top to bottom is essential, and devotes considerable space to rank-and-file employees and QC circles. Juran *et al.* (1974) and Crosby (1980) put less emphasis on the participation of all employees, although they clearly believe that far greater *managerial* participation is called for.

Juran maintains that the QC circle is a special case that works well in Japanese culture but is more problematic in the United States. Nevertheless, he advocates the incorporation of non-managerial employees into quality management. Drawing on the social science literature relating to work satisfaction, job redesign and morale, he suggests that special motivational issues must be addressed before low-level employees can participate effectively. Deming (1986) indicates it may be necessary to reduce direct supervision, eliminate work standards (quotas), allow people to regain their pride in workmanship, and create non-adversarial relationships before people at the bottom of Western companies will choose to participate in improving the performance of the business.

Employees' reluctance to participate in quality improvement programmes has limited some applications of quality management principles in Britain, as will be shown below in the discussion of quality circles. But the difficulties are not as great as some predicted. TQM goes with the grain of human nature, since people like to be able to influence what happens around them; most would also prefer to produce quality products rather than things they know are defective. The real issue is not employee resistance but the need for *management* to provide the right framework and modify its treatment of employees. Once management has changed its ways, then it can invite the involvement of other employees with a reasonable chance of success.

The great majority of contemporary schemes for total quality are built on the premise that success depends on the participation of all organizational members, from the most senior managers to the ordinary office or shop floor employee. This view reflects several assumptions. First, every person in the business has relevant knowledge and experience to contribute to the process of improving efficiency and effectiveness. Second, traditional managerial practices and organizational arrangements do not effectively harness this potential to contribute. Third, given the right setting most people welcome the opportunity to contribute to improving quality. Fourth, people are more likely to become committed to quality on a daily basis if they are involved in making the relevant decisions.

Widespread participation in decision-making for improvement is the key feature of the new method of management in an altogether different sense. That is, it represents for most companies a substantial change in the style of managing, a shift away from individual decision-making and authoritative, top-down communication, towards a more collective process with greater two-way communication and less emphasis on giving and receiving commands. In practice, the top management group of most companies has already learned to work as a team, but further down the managerial hierarchy the notion of teamwork has tended to be more rhetoric than substance. And people on the office and shop floor have always been excluded from any significant participation.

Sixth, establish a quality culture

The appropriate culture, shared widely, is the matrix that binds quality systems and structures together, makes participation possible and establishes quality improvement as the normal way of working. The appropriate culture has many elements, according to Ishikawa (1985) and Deming (1986):

1) The internalisation of quality and continuous improvement as a goal of all activities;

2) More open communications, so that those further down are listened to by those further up;

3) The greater involvement of a wider range of people in the decision-making process;

4) The development of high-trust social relationships, which are characterised by the abolition of adversarial and competitive

behaviour, by respect for individuals and by the lessening of cultural differences between managerial employees and others;

5)   A systematic, coherent and rational approach to improvement;

6)   The absolute priority of customer satisfaction.

Cultural change of this magnitude is of course very difficult for any organization to engineer. The central thrust of quality management is that people have to be managed in a particular way if their full contribution to the success of the business is to be realised. We should now look at the main people issues facing companies that decide to follow this route to enhanced performance.

The lessons of quality circles

The quality circle boom of the early and middle 1980s demonstrated that even small-scale participation in the quality process can contribute to efficient operations. Small groups of office and shop floor employees, all volunteers, trained in basic techniques of problem solving and typically led by first line supervisors, identified and solved a host of quality issues within their own work areas. The benefits of individual solutions were small but cumulatively could lead to fairly substantial improvements in the quality of work, with a tangible financial return. Some of the improvements affected working conditions and procedures that enhanced the comfort and safety of work; these changes improved employees' quality of work life and only indirectly fed through to business performance. Employers who established quality circles typically hoped to improve the quality of both operations and human relations. Encouraging rank-and-file participation was expected to improve morale, communications, relations with management, and employee commitment to the organization and its goals.

In two separate investigations during the early and late 1980s members of the Business Performance Group studied the application of quality circles in more than 20 British and American firms (Bradley and Hill, 1983, 1987; Hill, 1991a, 1991b). These studies suggested that while quality circles produced operational improvements, few gains were achieved in the area of human relations. Indeed, the results could be negative, if the circles raised aspirations which could not be satisfied (implementation of circle suggestions often depended on managerial approval, which was not always forthcoming) or if relations within a work group were soured by a division between circle members and their peers who did not join (as a rule, fewer than 10 per cent of eligible employees volunteered for membership).

A critical problem was that no organization was able to get the management of circles right. Although managerial culture contributed to this failure, it was rooted in the structure of circles. Circles were introduced by fairly senior managers, who then required middle managers to work with them. Among middle managers, we often found a lukewarm commitment to the idea of participative management in general and considerable misgivings about quality circles in particular. Many were uncomfortable with the idea of encouraging their subordinates to identify problems and solutions that they themselves had missed, which could make the managers look incompetent to their own superiors. Circles were particularly disliked because of their elaborate and formal procedures and because they were outside the control of the responsible manager.

Circle programmes set up a structure parallel to the normal chain of command. Members choose their own agenda of issues, which may not correspond with the priorities of the manager. They meet regularly at fixed times, regardless of how convenient this is to the normal work of the organization. They develop their own solutions and present them formally to management. Because of the presence of facilitators and senior management oversight, the circle manager is exposed to outside scrutiny. Managers often complain that circles deal with minor issues, and use managerial time that would more usefully be spent on other things, while regular meetings jeopardise output.

Managers further feel that they do not always get credit for the improvements made by their subordinates acting in their capacity as circle members. Not surprisingly, few managers feel ownership of their quality circles and the quality improvement process. Finally, some resent being obliged to allow their subordinates to participate when they themselves do not have similar rights *vis-a-vis* their own superiors.

Quality circles have highlighted a number of important issues in quality management. First and foremost, the quality improvement process must be properly integrated into the existing management structure and not organized separately. Managers need to feel ownership of the quality of their units, and understand that quality improvement is an integral part of normal management. They also need to feel that quality improvement is not a threat, and that the effectiveness, relevance and implementation of decisions are broadly within their control.

Second, quality improvement cannot be voluntary. If the participation of 10 per cent significantly improves quality, how much more could 100 per cent achieve! Voluntary participation sends two important signals: first, the company does not regard quality improvement as an integral aspect of everyone's job, but as something people opt into;

second, it does not intend to take sanctions against those who decline to pursue quality improvement.

Third, participation should extend upwards in the organization rather than be confined to those at the bottom.

Some commentators believe that circles are here to stay (eg, Collard & Dale, 1989). But we have found evidence that companies are moving on from circles in a number of ways. Some no longer bother with any structured quality improvement process; others have developed *quality improvement groups*. These groups are formed on an *ad hoc* basis to deal with a particular issue and are directed by the responsible manager. They are participative but do not cause the difficulties associated with circles; often they do not use the formal procedures that circles were trained to apply.

This approach can produce useful improvements and is certainly better than paying no real attention to quality, but it has major limitations. There is no assurance that individual managers will spot quality problems; the approach lacks the power that comes from having significant numbers of people trained and committed to look for improvement; and it concentrates more on efficiency than effectiveness and satisfying customers.

A small group of companies has pursued quality in a systematically structured and wide-ranging way, aiming at *total* quality. We have investigated two such organizations, both major international companies involved in office automation. The next section presents some of the important issues that emerge. (See Hill, 1991b, for a more detailed analysis of the findings.)

Total quality

The objective of the total quality process is to create a culture in which the pursuit of quality is accepted as the normal way of doing business, and the principles of managing for quality are applied so routinely that they become second nature. The objective may be simple, but reaching it is not.

Integration of quality improvement into management

In a full-scale system of *quality management* the structure of participation follows, and is integrated into, the existing structure of management. Quality improvement teams are formed at each level within the vertical line as part of the existing reporting system. Some teams comprise people of a single status; on others, bosses and subordinates jointly tackle improvement issues. Managers can also expect their subordinates individually to use the techniques of quality improvement in the performance of their normal tasks. In addition, special teams may be created to tackle issues that cut across the vertical structure of departments and functions.

Teams start by defining the mission and essential activities of their units, examining how well these tasks are performed, and consulting with their customers to see if their requirements are being met. Team members identify and implement solutions to quality problems that emerge from this process. Typically, many of the problems were already recognised, but had never been tackled. But many unanticipated quality problems are also discovered when a team takes a dispassionate look at what was previously taken for granted.

Quality gurus suggest that this major evaluation of activities should be repeated regularly. In practice companies do not seem to follow this advice. As quality management becomes more routine, there is a tendency to deal with problems as they become obvious – in a reactive manner – rather than to sit down and systematically appraise organizational activities from scratch.

In one of the companies we investigated, it was decided after several years of quality management that managers would have to lead major quality review sessions with their subordinates and customers at least once a year, in order to identify new quality issues and to demonstrate their commitment to improvement to those below.

The centrality of top management

Total quality is driven from the top. Top management in both companies we studied committed large sums of money to training – every person in each company received at least three days' training and many had much more – and much effort to pushing quality systems into place. Top management was the first group to be trained in and to implement the quality principles, which then cascaded down the organization. Top managers also acted as visible role models for those below.

Overcoming resistance and generating commitment

Quality management is never universally welcomed, and a minority of employees can be expected to react with passive resistance. Job security is always a concern, since greater efficiency will reduce the need for staff. The prospect of extra workloads does not appeal to everyone either, and quality management is indeed time consuming and mentally taxing. Others find participative management uncongenial. People have endured a fair number of management fads over the last twenty years and are sceptical that *Quality* will be any different. They tend to ask why they should put themselves out when the fad will surely pass.

Enthusiasts of quality management typically emphasise that top management holds the key to generating commitment further down in the organization. To this end, sensible managements will demonstrate that improving quality does not threaten jobs, but the other components of resistance are less easy to counter. The remedies proposed by management consultants selling quality packages comprise a mixture of propaganda and exhortation, demonstration and recognition. Quality management is talked up in public pronouncements and the company's internal channels of communication, top managers ostentatiously act as role models (at least for a while), and an apparatus of prizes and presentations is created to give recognition to outstanding achievements in the quality field.

But these methods lack power, at least on their own. To return to the lessons of Quality Circles, companies need to *integrate quality into the existing management structure* and they have to *ensure that it is obligatory*. The structuring of total quality efforts meets the first criterion, but the second does not automatically follow. In the companies we have studied, the consultants' solutions typically do not solve the problem; if quality management is not to be a option, it must be treated in the same way as other required elements of a manager's job. One company includes performance in following the quality principles as an element in its systems of appraisal and remuneration; quality is a consideration when promotions and dismissals are decided. In the other firm, senior establishment managers have been set numerical targets for the number of employees in quality improvement groups, and these attract financial bonuses. Top management in both companies tended to fight shy of this sort of development in the early years of their programmes for fear of creating ill will, but over time the necessity became clear.

Moreover, corporate management must consider the objectives it sets for its subsidiaries. If quality is of major concern at the corporate level, then this has to be recognised when the business priorities of subsidiaries are set. One company we studied has given customer satisfaction first place in its list of divisional objectives, ahead of return on assets and market share. This change was made after divisional management complained that corporate managers continually preached the importance of meeting customer requirements but employed different criteria in running the business.

Top management is the most powerful group in any organization, with the greatest influence over how people behave, but it has to use this power in a relevant and down-to-earth way. Propaganda and trinkets are not enough. The task of top managers is to use the correct incentives to ensure that quality management does indeed become routine rather than peripheral.

Middle management

We have noticed a shift in the centre of gravity of quality activity over time. There is a tendency for middle managers and technical and professional staff to become the main participants, for teams that run horizontally across the hierarchy rather than vertically through units to become more numerous, and for senior managers to participate less. Senior managers identify problems, which they delegate to teams of subordinates, but they do not actively practice the principles of quality management themselves. They do, however, continue to oversee the administration of their quality systems. Managers at lower levels find the sorts of issues that need to be tackled by special project teams more interesting and important. They know that successful performance here will bring them to the attention of more senior managers, and they benefit from broadening their understanding of the company. People at the bottom continue to solve problems within the limits of their competence, but there is a risk that they may lose sight of the bigger issues and the sense of recognition that more input from their managers would bring.

Because these two companies were relatively successful in institutionalising the search for quality improvement even on the office and shop floors, they tended to assume that, once established, quality procedures would become self-perpetuating and require no reinforcement. In fact, as both companies now recognise, quality efforts need continual stimulation; hence in one case managers were obliged to form an *improvement team* with subordinates each year; in the other company they set numerical targets.

Outcomes

It is always difficult to identify a cultural change, but there are indications that a quality culture was becoming established in both companies we studied. Measurable outcomes of the quality process, such as greater customer satisfaction reduced, non-conformance and reduced costs of quality, showed that the companies' performance was improving. These outcomes suggested that something had changed inside the organizations, while the companies' own surveys of employee opinion showed that most people had absorbed elements of a quality culture, saw the necessity of improvement and rated other people in the company favourably in terms of their commitment to quality.

The scale of quality activity in dynamic companies can be immense. The management literature includes many examples of huge cost savings resulting from the introduction of quality management systems. While such figures are undoubtedly important, they are not a definitive guide. There is always a temptation to inflate the numbers to present a worthy course of action in the best light. Moreover, many of the benefits of quality are not capable of this sort of quantification. No one doubts, for example, that poor quality costs a company new and repeat business, but it is virtually impossible to measure these lost sales accurately.

Looking at quality initiatives provides a different idea of the magnitude and scope of this activity. In one company we studied, a single division employing 5000 people had 600 quality improvement projects under way at various times in the course of a year (the fourth year of the quality improvement process), which indicates a real depth of commitment to quality. Some of these improvements were the result of months of effort by specially convened interdepartmental and multi-functional project teams, others were the product of a few hours' work among colleagues in the same office or workplace. Some were precisely and realistically measured, others were soft at the edges, a few could scarcely be measured at all. The measurable benefits of one initiative were in excess of £1 million, but most were much smaller.

The search for quality has to be tested against measurable criteria wherever possible. But if quality management is to become a way of life, then the *spirit* of quality needs to be nurtured as well as the mentality of the accountant. There will always be times when the spirit proceeds on the basis of judgement tinged with faith.

Conclusion

Companies that embark on quality management are committing themselves to a long and difficult endeavour. At the outset, quality management can yield significant improvements, simply because there is so much slack in most firms. Over time, however, as the easy sources of improvement are exhausted, improvement becomes more difficult and proceeds in smaller steps. Moreover, the goal posts of quality keep moving, as customers and competition continually redefine the standards of fitness that will prevail.

If the principles of quality management are to become internalised as the normal way of running a company, the culture of the business and its members will normally need to change. This too is a long drawn-out process: the two companies investigated here reckon that it takes five to seven years to engineer the required change, even with a constant population of employees. Given staff turnover and new hirings, there will always be a need for training and socialisation into quality principles. TQM, therefore, is not a *programme* or a change package that companies can install and then forget. Rather it represents a different way of organizational life, and needs continual servicing and development to succeed.

The human resource implications of TQM look increasingly attractive to companies that are already facing shortages of people with certain sorts of competence; recruitment and retention can only become more difficult in the later 1990s, as demographic change reshapes the structure of the labour force in Britain. Quality management obviously economises on people by increasing their efficiency. Equally significant is the Japanese experience that TQM contributes to *people building*, by raising their levels of motivation and morale and enhancing their skills. This suggests that the cultural change and individual development aspects of quality management could help companies to raise the competence of their employees and increase their chances of attracting and keeping staff.

There is as yet no solid evidence from British companies that the Japanese experience will be repeated, although quality management enthusiasts in many firms believe that such human resource development is indeed under way. But this outcome seems quite plausible on *a priori* grounds. The social science literature relating to work motivation and organizational loyalty suggests there is considerable value in greater autonomy on the job, more input into decision-making, more teamworking and a wider range of social interaction at work. In addition, the quality management emphasis on systematic training and learning through doing, with staff required to tackle quality improvement issues they would previously have ignored or left to others, is likely to raise the general level of competence within an organization.

At best, however, the potential of TQM in the human resource area will be realised only slowly. These gains will come as a result of a considerable cultural change within organizations, which will itself take many years to complete.

10

Management Accounting and the Measurement of Business Performance: Some Dilemmas

Eamonn Walsh

Business performance

Accounting systems attempt to measure business performance. But business performance is a dynamic concept and its definition changes over time. For example, contemporary pleas for better performance are frequently couched in terms of international competitiveness. This in itself is not new especially in the United Kingdom. Much of the debate about the control of inflation was conducted in the name of international competitiveness, with comparisons of local and overseas labour costs. More recently the focus has shifted from labour costs to other dimensions of international competitiveness, such as achieving a comparative advantage in manufacturing and in marketing skills. Performance is now perceived as closely related to the adoption of modern manufacturing technologies and objectives (eg, quality, zero inventories, the ownership of international brand names and marketing expertise).

Accepting that modern manufacturing technologies and marketing skills are key dimensions of business performance, the next step is to examine the interplay between these factors and accounting. After a brief explanation of how accountants measure performance, we will see how accounting may impede the development of these dimensions of business performance.

A partial, imperfect accounting primer

Accounting has its origins in bookkeeping: the recording of economic transactions which arise from transfers of cash or agreements to transfer cash. From this data accounting produces periodic statements of income and balance sheets. To draw up an income statement, one must decide how revenue should be recognised and then attach (or match) expenses to these revenues. Generally, revenues are recognised when:

1) Performance is substantially complete (eg, goods or services have been delivered to a customer).

2) Revenue has been realized (eg, goods and services are exchanged for cash or claims to cash).

Accounting conventions ensure that revenues are recognised for a given period and product expenses are matched with those revenues. Period costs are matched with a specific period, and income is determined by deducting product and period costs from revenues obtained during the period. Product expenses are the cost of assets sold to customers and period expenses are those which are difficult or costly to relate to the revenues. For example, a retailer might treat the cost of merchandise purchased as a *product* expense, and the cost of sales staff as a *period* expense. Furthermore, it might be necessary to estimate certain expenses, but this, in principle, is straightforward. However, producing periodic income statements from such transactions can cause difficulties since they may display substantial discrepancies between flows of income and flows of cash.

During the life of an enterprise such differences arise and these can give misleading signals of business performance. Fixed assets are one. Accountants treat fixed assets as economic resources arising from past transactions, which will benefit more than one accounting period. Their costs, therefore, should be allocated over several accounting periods. For example, if a typewriter with a useful life of, say, five years is purchased for £100, its costs may be depreciated at a rate of £20 per annum over five years. The total cost of the asset (the cash flow) is equal to the total amount of the expense during the five year period. However, during those five years, the *expense* flow differs from the *cash* flow, and further, the expense flow need not bear any relationship whatsoever to the flow of services obtained from the asset.

In summary, the calculation of accounting performance, also known as *accounting income*, is based upon a revenue recognition principle, and attempts to match expenses with revenues earned in a meaningful way. Expenses which are difficult or costly to match with revenues are treated as period expenses, and charged against revenue in the period in which they occur. Furthermore, accounting is based upon economic transactions which give rise to exchanges of cash. These accounting conventions have some severe limitations when it comes to measuring the performance of a business.

How well did we do?

A simple example demonstrates the point. Suppose that Alpha Corporation has been working on a revolutionary new software package which has successfully undergone testing; initial reviews have been excellent and the company is looking forward to a successful launch of its new product. Development and testing have taken six months, at a cost of £5m. Alpha has also recruited a first rate sales force, and it expects that sales of its new product will begin in the next accounting period. The potential market for the product is estimated at £100m in the first twelve months of trading.

A competitor, the Omega Corporation sells a product which will be rendered obsolete by Alpha's new product. Omega's sales force has announced that it intends to leave to join the Alpha Corporation. At the beginning of the current accounting period, Omega's research team defected to Alpha and were not replaced. This resulted in a cost saving for the Omega Corporation of £5m. During the same accounting period Omega sold £30m of software, at a cost of £3m.

Common sense would suggest that the Alpha Corporation had benefitted substantially at the expense of the Omega Corporation. However, accounting numbers suggest a completely different view. In the case which I have described the Omega Corporation would record net income of £27m and Alpha's results would be somewhere between a £5m *loss* and breakeven, depending upon the accounting rules adopted. Therefore if accounting income were the sole performance criterion, Alpha is a lemon and Omega is a rising star. This erroneous conclusion arises from the failure of accounting statements to take account of intangible economic benefits arising from cash transactions, and their failure to recognise that some economic events do not result in cash flows in the current accounting period.

For example, the beneficial outcome of Alpha's research is not recognised as current period revenue. More seriously, accounting rules may require the company to treat the £5m research and development expenditure as an immediate *expense* rather than as an intangible *asset*. Conversely, although the departure of Omega's research staff represents the loss of an extremely valuable, intangible asset, it is treated by the accounting system as a benefit (eg, a £5m cash saving). The accounting view of the business also fails to recognise the loss of Omega's sales force – another valuable human resource – and the imminent obsolescence of the company's product. Furthermore the accounting system does not give any credit to the Alpha Corporation for its recruitment of Omega's sales force.

This is a contrived and oversimplified example, and accounting results are not necessarily so misleading but it does raise some important questions: are the relevant dimensions of performance captured by accounting in a timely manner? Are flows of cash and claims to cash closely coupled with economic events in a temporal sense? In general, if an organization's activities are dominated by stochastic, complex, long-term processes, accounting will be a poor index of performance. Examples of such biasing activities might include expenditures on training, quality, software and process development, research, and marketing activities which usually involve a crucial human dimension. Thus an organization might find it more useful to employ performance measures that focus directly on these dimensions, such as outcomes of training programmes, attitudes to quality and the number of customer complaints.

What are we good at?

Many companies' accounting systems yield figures for the cost of particular products that are based upon inventory valuations. Often the inventory values reflect the full cost of the product: both direct costs of production and overheads, which are allocated to individual products. Table 10.1 gives an example of a pen factory that makes two product lines, blue pens and red ones. By allocating total factory overhead costs between the two product lines – here on the basis of direct labour hours – it is possible to arrive at a cost per unit for each product line.

Table 10.1 Breakdown of production costs: Full costing

	Red product line	Blue product line
Daily production	200,000 units	800,000 units
Direct materials	£0.1	£0.12
Direct labour	£0.1	£0.1
Direct labour hours	0.0001 hrs	0.0001 hrs
Factory overhead	£500,000	£500,000
Alloc. overhead	£0.5	£0.5
Unit cost	£0.7	£0.72
selling price	£1	£1
Profit per unit	£0.3	£0.28
Total profit	£60,000	£224,000

Accounting academics warn that great care is needed in using the type of information contained in table 10.1 as a basis for making business decisions. For example, suppose our company receives a special order for 100,000 pens (either red or blue) at £0.21 per pen. On the basis of full costs, the company should reject the order, since the price is far less than the full cost of the pens. If the company has spare capacity, however, its overheads may not be increased by accepting this order; then the *relevant* cost for this decision is the *marginal* or *additional* cost of producing 100,000 pens. An analysis based on marginal costs, shown in table 10.2, indicates that accepting the order for 100,000 red pens will add £1,000 to profits.

Table 10.2 Breakdown of production costs: Marginal costing

	Red product line	Blue product line
Direct materials	£0.1	£0.12
Direct labour	£0.1	£0.1
Marginal cost	£0.2	£0.22
Tender price	£0.21	£0.21
Contribution per unit	£0.01	-£0.01
Contribution 100k units	£1,000	-£1,000

Recently, critics have argued that this approach treats overheads as a *black box*, and that both traditional full costing and marginal costing may be misleading. They point out that in contemporary manufacturing settings, direct labour has become a much less significant component of costs, and therefore may distort true product costs when used as a basis for allocating overheads. They also note the significance of cost drivers other than volume and the increasing size of the black box relative to total costs.

Activity Based Costing (ABC) is one alternative approach. ABC involves breaking plant level costs down into individual product line costs, and then breaking product line costs down into *product sustaining activities* (eg, process engineering, product movements, purchase orders, inspection, etc) and *unit level activities* (eg, direct labour, materials etc). ABC aims to identify the factors (number of units, batches, or products, rather than the number of units alone) which drive or influence the size of the black box.

Suppose analysis reveals that part of our pen factory overhead lies in *product line related activities*. Thus, as table 10.3 shows, an entirely different impression of product profitability emerges. It becomes clear that the cost of producing a red pen exceeds its selling price. Such an analysis might lead the company to drop the red product line and to focus on blue pens alone (table 10.4).

The ABC approach is still in its infancy, and more research is necessary to establish its applicability to a wide variety of manufacturing situations. However, it has the advantage of focusing attention on the

Table 10.3 Breakdown of production costs: Activity based costing

	Red product line	Blue product line
Daily production	200,000 units	800,000 units
Direct materials	£0.1	£0.12
Direct labour	£0.1	£0.1
Direct labour hours	0.0001 hrs	0.0001 hrs
Product overhead	£200,000	£200,000
Prod. O/H per unit	£1	£0.25
Product level cost	£1.2	£0.47
Factory overhead	£100,000	£100,000
Alloc. overhead	£0.1	£0.1
Unit (full) cost	£1.3	£0.57
Selling price	£1	£1
Profit per unit	-£0.3	£0.43
Total profit	-£60,000	£344,000

Table 10.4 Benefits arising from concentrating on blue product line

	Blue product line
Daily production	800,000 units
Direct materials	£0.12
Direct labour	£0.1
Direct labour hours	0.0001 hrs
Product overhead	£200,000
Factory overhead	£100,000
Prod. O/H per unit	£0.25
Alloc. overhead	£0.125
Unit cost	£0.595
Selling price	£1
Profit per unit	£0.405
Total profit	£324,000

	Total profit
Both products	£304,000
Both prods + order	£305,000
One product	£324,000

black box, and enables more thoughtful analyses of product profitability. It is likely to be of greatest value in situations where overheads constitute a significant proportion of total costs.

Accounting as an impediment to performance

In addition to some of the problems I have discussed, accounting may also play a role in reinforcing organizational hierarchies. Departments are frequently defined in accounting terms and accounting numbers may be used to analyse departmental performance. This can create special problems beyond those already described. Similarly, capital expenditures, which can be important to future business performance, may be controlled using a variety of quantitative techniques.

Departmental performance

Many modern organizations are organized into profit and cost centres, a structure enabled and reinforced by accounting measurement. The creation of these subdivisions may significantly affect certain dimensions of performance. A company concerned with improving quality, for example, may find that the establishment of profit and cost centres creates perverse incentives, especially when the costs of quality are borne by one department while its benefits are credited to another. For example, a purchasing department which buys substandard materials may be praised for achieving cost savings. Down the line, however, the costs of using inferior materials are borne by other departments. Similarly, bonuses based on *output* may encourage employees in a sub-assembly department to work too fast, so that they produce a high quantity of substandard work. In such a situation it is not uncommon for the rework costs to be borne by another department or viewed as an overhead.

Capital budgeting

Capital budgeting techniques (eg, Payback and Net Present Value) involve some attempt to quantify the costs and benefits of proposed investments as an aid to decision making. If investment decisions are based upon these calculations alone, then the non-quantifiable or qualitative consequences of proposed projects will be ignored. Proponents of new manufacturing technologies (eg, Computer Aided Manufacturing and Flexible Manufacturing Systems) argue that the failure to incorporate qualitative factors may discriminate against newer manufacturing technologies since many of the benefits of these technologies are inherently unquantifiable. Examples of these benefits might include flexibility, learning and long term competitive disadvantage especially if competitors adopt these technologies. While this argument has a certain intuitive appeal, it ignores many of the unquantifiable costs associated with these technologies including organizational disruption, training, learning and unforeseen problems in its operationalisation (see chapter 11 for a discussion of problems associated with technology and information systems). Ultimately, investing by numbers is likely to result in poor decisions, regardless of the technologies under consideration.

Conclusions

In the last decade many accountants, especially in the Unites States, increasingly have become concerned that management accounting may hamper companies' adaptation to new realities. First, it is argued that *quantitative* investment appraisal techniques discriminate against the adoption of new manufacturing technologies that are critical to competitiveness, because many of their benefits are unquantifiable. Less is heard of the unquantifiable costs associated with these technologies.

Critics charge that accounting systems reflect the changing cost structure of manufacturing but direct costs now constitute a much smaller proportion of total costs. This leaves an even larger residual – the black box – to which accountants pay comparatively little attention. Recent research has indicated new ways of analysing this black box in order to produce more helpful cost analyses.

Traditional accounting models are poorly equipped to deal with intangible assets, which have become increasingly important in business. Human resources are a case in point. The urge to produce immediate visible cost savings led many British firms to lay off skilled employees during the recession of the early 1980s – a decision they lived to regret during the boom years at the end of the decade. Many companies responded similarly to the economic downturn of the early 1990s. This is totally inappropriate during times of tight labour markets and an increasing demand for skills (see chapter 12).

Finally, accounting enables a mode of organization (subdivision of the enterprise into profit and cost centres) that may prove to be counterproductive. While it is difficult to argue with the creation of quasi-market forces within organizations, it is worrying that these same forces may create externalities which are difficult to internalise. The creation of internal economies which exclude quality and improvements in human resources may cause those same economies to crumble when exposed to external market forces.

11

Management Information Systems: Opportunity or Risk?

Ian Angell

Introduction

The efficiency gains that can be realised, at least in theory, through information technology (IT) are widely discussed. Less often acknowledged, unfortunately, are the risks and limitations of these technologies. Many organizations are now built around a complex network of interconnected information systems whose functioning is well understood by only a handful of people. The reliance on a few such individuals poses several kinds of risk, of which sabotage is only the most dramatic.

Sound technological decisions require systematic attention to human considerations. This chapter develops a checklist of questions for managers which will help them to identify the opportunities and risks inherent in the applications of new technologies.

Emerging problems and disillusion

Over the last three decades, virtually every sector of business and society has confidently promoted computerisation rather than studying it critically. The prevailing view has been that the benefits of computerisation are self-evident, and that any problems are minor and soluble. The popular media have insinuated images of benign machinery solving organizational problems: mass consumption television programmes trumpet the merits of microcomputers, promotional videos make business people feel inadequate without the latest computerised management methods, and magazines and specialist pages of newspapers equate technology with innovation. Some governments have viewed computer education as essential for future commercial success achieved through the prudent and benevolent application of machines, information, measurement and mathematical logic.

Such optimism is misguided. Already people are becoming disillusioned with technology because it often fails to deliver benefits commensurate with the huge investments required, and because of its damaging side-effects. In fact, it has been estimated that only 5 per cent of ordered software is actually used (shelf ware), and that 29 per cent of the software that has been paid for is never even delivered (United States General Accounting Office, 1979). For most of the past decade managers have claimed that their greatest headache is meeting IT project deadlines (Price Waterhouse, 1989-90). Meanwhile, it has been estimated that ten million programmers will be needed worldwide in 1990, at an estimated annual cost of $250 billion (Boehm, 1988). The question of value for money is becoming ever more important; we are paying more for less, and the cost of saving with technology is often greater than the savings themselves.

> 'In the mid 1980s, top management made a determined stand against runaway cost escalation unjustified by business improvements. Data processing management responded during the latter part of the 1980s by instituting more effective performance measurements and cost controls. The evidence for this is now clear. What is not clear, however, is whether actual and predicted upturns mark a return to the bad old days, when budgets were driven up by capacity problems – or whether the new management controls are, in fact, working, and the increased spend reflects value for money.' (Price Waterhouse, 1989-90)

Instead of simplifying organizational tasks, computers often precipitate and promote production bottlenecks and lead to an increased complexity which can culminate in an incomprehensible electronic bureaucracy and a logorrhea of computer jargon. The KISS advice – *Keep It Simple, Stupid* – (Weizenbaum, 1976), is seldom remembered in the grandiose schemes of managers and politicians. Instead of developing a coherent policy linking technological development to corporate goals, companies tend to surrender responsibility for IT to technocrats who indulge their own fascination with irrelevant technological fads without considering the wider strategic needs of the organization.

Managers need to shift their attention from narrow functional issues to an understanding of how information technology can enhance a company's competitive position. Furthermore, a sensitivity to the broader human issues is essential for the successful integration of IT and corporate strategies (Price Waterhouse, 1988-89). If we are not careful, the enthusiastic acceptance of information technology will soon be replaced by alienation, distrust, disillusion and resentment in many sectors of business and society.

Reconsider priorities: the fundamental place of people

The arbitrary application of computers poses significant societal and organizational risks. Instead of regarding information as a problem of machines, we need to look at organizational information systems as social systems, in which people – employees, customers and suppliers – play the fundamental roles.

The design of information systems should begin with an understanding of the context, the purpose and the meaning of information, and only then move on to such issues as the form and methods of communication, implementation, application, evaluation, justification and management. Such an approach is necessarily multi-disciplinary, so that the effective use of communication and computer technologies is based firmly in the social sciences. The use of machinery cannot be separated from human intellect, aspirations, culture, philosophy and social organization. Even IT, therefore, must leave room for intuition, insight, inspiration and lateral thinking.

What can't be counted, doesn't count

The application of computer technology has encouraged a quantitative approach to problem solving and management. Seeking greater efficiency and effectiveness, many organizations have relied too heavily on naive performance measures, which can distort incentives. Automation of these measures just makes things worse. All the creative energies of the organization are geared towards maximising the measure scores, instead of the true organizational purpose. Such measure-driven practices are likely to create long term problems and systems failure.

Limits of *scientific* management

Not every problem has an algorithmic and quantitative solution. In fact, when the *solutions* that emerge from the software laboratories are imposed on an actual organization, the results can be disruptive (Checkland, 1981; Tate, 1988). We have been too quick to apply scientific, statistical and technological methods without asking whether they are truly appropriate. Often scientific management is no more than the wishful projection of past trends and structures onto a complex and uncertain future. This approach virtually guarantees that we will misinterpret emergent realities, and miss new opportunities.

Organizational structure must change if companies are to make the most of their human and technological resources. It is the human beings that will recognise unusual events as emergent opportunities and risks, and they must be able to take radical and innovative action in response. If companies insist on enforcing a measurement imperative, then the human resource will simply mimic the machine, and all is lost. *The real danger is not that machines will become like man, but that man will become like machines.*

IT in the organization: Bureaucracies and power

Companies must come to grips not only with the importance of IT within their organizations, but also with its limitations. In particular, they must resolve the position of the IT executive within the corporate hierarchy. It is claimed that by the mid 1990s, 63 per cent of United Kingdom Chief Executive Officers intend to make IT a full board level appointment, (Price Waterhouse, 1988-89). Such a position requires a broad, subtle strategic view of IT applications within companies (with primary focus on information rather than technology), and an understanding of the fundamental role that alert and free-thinking employees will play in this future. Many of the technocrats now produced by educational systems, think in terms of machines replacing people and are unsuited for such responsibility.

In addition to investing (appropriately) in technology, companies need to put greater emphasis on a policy for the effective management and use of personnel at all levels in the organization. Such a policy should not only inject realism into expectations for the benefits of technology, but release the potential fount of ideas and innovation in the workforce as a whole. To do this, we need to understand how technological systems affect both business and individual performance.

Computers can either simplify or complicate matters. We must learn when to use automated systems and performance measures, and when they should be scrapped before they become liabilities (usually because of non-technological factors). The enormous cost of developing systems often creates a bureaucratic power base with so much inertia that the system continues far beyond its useful life; the company cannot bear to write off such a large capital investment. Eventually, however, the commercial situation may have changed so radically that the system will cause the organization to be uncompetitive. When that time comes (or preferably even earlier), we need to have the confidence to change our minds.

Strategic thinking about IT

In the future, information technology is likely to undermine the infrastructure of many vested interest groups, within individual organizations, nationally and internationally. The major issue for the next decade is how to manage these changes with some semblance of confidence. Decisions must not be based on technological fashions. Aggrandised management information systems (Ackoff, 1967), little more than computerised executive toys, should not be allowed to replace effective qualitative management, and the real benefits of systems simplification must not be overlooked.

Strategic management is the preparation and disposition of resources within an organization, enabling it to contend with its commerical rivals and with the uncertainty and complexity inherent in an unknown future. Unless the context of information is fully appreciated, and the true nature of crisis, complexity and uncertainty recognised, strategies will become wishful thinking.

Investing in human resources

In the future, the major impact of information technology will not be in software or hardware. It will be in: (i) the linking of information technology to a more efficient industrial and commercial base, (ii) in enhanced human-to-human communication, and (iii) in the application and sale of expertise and information itself. It is the human factor, not technology, that makes the difference between commercial success and failure, and between acceptance and rejection of a system. Hence the wealth of a country (the true asset of a company) is its educated population (employees); they are the real strategic resource essential for commercial growth and the essence of sustained competitive advantage.

Companies need to concentrate not only on finding out who the best people are and how to attract them, but on how to train, assign, motivate, and retain them. In the mid 1980s, 'Barclays Bank ran 12 recruitment drives which netted only 100 new computer specialists, 97 of whom were lost to different companies within the next year.' (Leadbeater and Lloyd, 1987)

It is through an investment in people that companies can become information rich and create an atmosphere of enthusiasm and purposeful innovation; without that investment, they are likely to misuse, misunderstand or mismanage information. Making the most of our human resources will require a long term investment in education, not just an accumulation of vocational skills. Vocational skills look into the *cul-de-sac* of a closed technological environment, whereas education gives an intellectual platform on which to base decisions about the management of crisis, complexity and change.

Artificial or human intelligence

As we begin to recognise the value, and the scarcity, of human expertise, it is not surprising that attempts are being made to develop artificial intelligence. Capital can no longer demand control of know-how companies (Sveilby and Lloyd, 1987). The individual expert, capital's old ally when using automation against organized labour, now poses a far greater threat. Great claims are being made for Expert Systems (Feigenbaum *et al.*, 1988) and other computerised techniques, but it is very doubtful whether they demonstrate anything other than the 'first step fallacy' (Dreyfus and Dreyfus, 1986). It is possible that the companies which introduce Expert Systems actually lose expertise, because they sacrifice the holistic understanding of human implications when building the rule base. By institutionalising an unjustified confidence, they inhibit the creation of the next generation of human experts – perhaps believing they will not need them!

Attempts to use technology to *take out the woolliness* are doomed to failure, because woolliness is an integral part of business life, and complete specification is not always possible. Automating processes may introduce a further level of complexity that obscures our lack of understanding and denies our uncertainty in those processes; if so, we are creating an accident waiting to happen.

The very existence of the human species demonstrates our success in dealing with the vagaries of the future. It makes no sense to submit the decisions that affect commercial success to simplistic rules and measurement, implemented on a glorified adding machine. 'Perfection of planning is a symptom of decay.' (Parkinson, 1986)

IT in its proper place

When used to enhance (rather than replace) intellect, information systems can be useful tools and can provide a framework for coping with future innovations, trends and requirements, and minimising dangers. But unquestioning acceptance of their models and simulations of open-ended human experience is sheer folly. In many business situations, for example, engineering principles and measurement are inappropriate because of differences in the perspectives (each valid in its own way) of customers, suppliers and employees.

Commercial and social pressures, cultural incompatibilities, chaotic changes, resistance to change, unpredictable accidents, malice and sabotage should also be considered in technological decisions. The accidents at Three Mile Island in the United States (Gall, 1988) and Chernobyl in the Soviet Union have demonstrated the fallacy of relying on fail-safe systems, rational methods of measurement, and simplistic calculations of the probabilities for system failure.

Information technology can create totally new commercial opportunities and possibly institutionalise structured knowledge, but it can also relegate decision-making to artificial (eg, alien) intelligences, undermine quality control, weaken security, lay an organization open to attack from competitors, and even destabilise it. On a relatively small scale adolescent pranks such as computer viruses have evolved into deliberate acts of industrial sabotage. No computer system is immune to *Homo sapiens*, the ultimate computer virus. The whole question of computer security and of more general emergent risk must be seen in a much broader social perspective.

Conclusion

Advances in computer technology are rapidly outstripping our ability to use and manage them, and they can prove highly counter-productive. We need to take a hard look at the behaviourial phenomena surrounding the use of computers in organizations. Even well-engineered designs can fail when training is poor, when the context changes, or when the unexpected occurs. The emphasis should not be on what systems can be built with a certain technology, but on whether they are appropriate and relevant, and in particular, whether it is possible to control them after they have been introduced into organizations and society in general. Will information technology cause its own forms of environmental, intellectual and social pollution? When we look at the values behind this technology will we find entropy mortgaging the future for short-term gains?

Managers must concentrate on the concepts which stand behind the use of information technology and look for imaginative approaches to future-oriented problems, both theoretical and tangible. By focusing on the *human* conceptual and organizational problems of the development and management of information systems, managers can place technology within an appropriate social context. This turns on its head the hitherto unsuccessful mind-set of technology, and promises to lead to a more effective approach.

Managers must understand the risks, as well as the opportunities, inherent in information technology applications. They must try to put them into an eclectic framework, one that includes social and organizational considerations as well as the technological, before trusting the future to this technology.

12

Profit-Related Pay: A Strategic Instrument for the 1990s

Greg Clark

One of the hallmarks of the 1980s was a recognition by corporate strategists of the need to survive in increasingly turbulent conditions. Markets became more competitive, competition more global. In turn the global market allowed boom and slump to be transmitted quickly around the world. With widely fluctuating exchange rates and interest rates, a year could see a profitable plant turned into a loss maker. The world became a less predictable environment in which to do business.

Transmitted to the organization of the firm, companies were encouraged to retrench into a core workforce resilient to changing conditions, and to develop a set of peripheral employees who could be taken up or set down as conditions demanded, whether through direct employment or subcontracting for specific functions. The greater flexibility of employing part-time workers, with limited rights to benefits and redundancy settlements, made hiring and firing easier, as did the increasing use of temporary workers. A new model of personnel management was adopted, characterised by flexibility. Where a firm was required to adjust quickly to an external pressure, it could effect the necessary changes in its workforce quickly and efficiently.

This 1980s response to the need for flexibility was appropriate at a time when the supply of labour was abundant. Continuing to pursue such a strategy today, however, can seriously compromise the ability of companies to recruit and retain their workforce and endow it with the skills which will be the key to success in the 1990s.

Just as the need for flexibility fashioned a new model for management in the 1980s, so a growing recognition of the competitive advantage in people can be detected in the early 1990s. Having made important headway in strategic focusing and market positioning in the past few years (eg, the company's *external* strategy), managers are now shifting their attention to the considerable gains to be made from a more coherent organization of the firm; its *internal* strategy.

As with the drive for flexibility, much of the initial pressure has come from the outside world. Demographic pressures, skills shortages and the need to raise skill levels are forcing the internal strategy onto senior managers' agendas.

Without a substantial unforeseen increase in the participation rate of the population, the supply of labour to most Western European companies will contract significantly in the years ahead (see chapter 3). While downturns in business can mitigate the problem from time to time, the underlying trends mean that companies can no longer depend on a ready supply of labour: if they are to maintain a high quality workforce and avoid the costs and disruption associated with high staff turnover rates they must place a new emphasis on recruitment and particularly retention as part of an internal strategy.

On top of the demands made by demographic change, there has come a new realisation of the importance of raising the skills level of the workforce. A striking feature of the new technology introduced into Britain in recent years is that it has increased the demand for skilled labour, confounding predictions that technical advance would be associated with a deskilled labour force. Automation may lead to less demanding tasks, but it requires a technically adept and literate workforce to control it. As companies, in response to labour shortages, substitute capital for labour, this demand for skilled technical workers is likely to become accentuated.

Competition from Europe redoubles this skills requirement. The skills level of the British workforce lags substantially behind its principal West European competitors, whether as a result of our largely non-vocational education system or the low level of in-service training supplied of British employers. Furthermore, British firms look set to be squeezed from the other end by new East European competitors, whose low skills levels are reflected in their labour costs. If British firms choose the low skills route they face a painful squeeze on margins to remain competitive. More palatable will be attempting to join the higher level of European Community producers, and this will require a raising of skills levels.

Though prompted by demographic and skills pressure, the new emphasis on people, and the opportunities in internal strategy, need not only be reactive. A belated recognition of the value which has always been inherent in people is increasingly being made in companies: many service sector companies hold scarcely any other asset than their skilled and experienced workforce. Generating even small percentage gains in productivity through more enlightened deployment of its workers is being seen as financially very lucrative for companies. The lack of attention paid to the human side of firms in the past is partly a reaction to the traditional reporting system. Accounting numbers, accepted as corporate targets, become management practice. Yet the accounting framework was laid down at a time when the British economy was dominated by low-skilled manufacturing, and it adopted the conventions appropriate to that. Thus while expenditure on capital equipment is expressed as an investment, sums devoted to training, the development of *human capital*, are considered a current cost. In times of financial stringency, therefore, training was the first to be squeezed, often to the detriment of the long term health of the company. The real cost of ignoring the human side has become glaring (see chapter 10).

Take as an example a case highlighted in work undertaken by the Business Performance Group. A company researchers investigated had a pool of 5,000 employees viewed by management as key to the company's future success. Each year £8,000 per individual was spent on training. The average tenure of a pool member was five years. Thus, the typical employee had at least £40,000 worth of the company's capital invested in him when he left. Dropping a modest 5 per cent of the workforce during a downturn to ease the wage bill wastes the capital accrued in 250 people: a sum of over £2 million. The more highly-trained the workforce has to be in the future, the more this loss will grow.

Corporate managers would not lightly scrap up-to-date capital equipment worth £2 million in a recession, especially if the downturn were expected to be relatively short lived. Companies which are prepared to take a more imaginative approach to managing their human capital, especially in recession, can unlock a major and underexploited source of long term competitive advantage. Recognising the competitive advantage in people – their contribution to productivity, the role of skills in strategic positioning, the opportunities in effective management of the resources invested in them – brings human resources into the ambit of strategic management. A strategy for the human aspects of the firm, an *internal* strategy, is taking its place alongside the *external* strategies devised in the past. For a strategy to have any value, however, other policies of the firm must be consistent with it, and certainly not act to undermine it.

If a more comprehensive view is taken of the value of human assets, which in turn leads to a positive place for them in an internal strategy, the high variability in numbers employed which characterised the 1980s may not only be incompatible with the strategy but actually destroy it. Basing a policy to achieve flexibility on dropping workers under adverse trading conditions, and expecting to pick them up again when conditions improve, clearly conflicts with a strategy involving raising skills levels and hence investing in human assets over the medium and long term. The loosening of workers' ties to the company through temporary, part-time and sub-contracted work runs the risk of being associated more with the hectic turnover than with valuable flexibility.

Yet the need for flexibility persists. The Gulf War and recession of the early 1990s remind us of the turbulence of current times. Firms must continue to brace themselves to respond to potential turbulence by building in strategic and operational flexibility. The workforce cannot avoid being targeted for flexibility. What is needed is an alternative way to incorporate flexibility into labour, so helping companies cope with an uncertain environment. But it must allow them to meet the challenge of retaining and increasing skills.

This situation calls for a number of solutions to be considered, and for new reporting tools to be devised to counteract a relative dearth of information relating to issues of internal strategy. This will allow better informed, and thus more sensitive management of human resources, bringing it more into the ambit of general corporate managers.

One specific strategic tool commends itself already through reason and evidence as being of possible benefit to managers in the years ahead: profit-related pay.

Faced with pressure to achieve a 5 per cent reduction in the wage bill, the company in our example mentioned above could make 250 of its employees redundant. However, we have seen that this is tantamount to scrapping £2 million of its accrued human capital; a figure which, augmented by redundancy costs (though these are often treated as exceptional items below the line) could be detrimental to the company's medium and long term well being. An alternative way to achieve the same cost savings from the wage bill is to implement a 5 per cent dip in wages and salaries.

Companies can introduce flexibility to their wage bill in two ways. To maintain a stable wage for those employed, but vary the number of workers employed; or to support a relatively stable workforce and allow pay to fluctuate.

British employers have traditionally opted for the former approach. Yet this means that, in the words of former Chancellor of the Exchequer Nigel Lawson:

> 'If the only element of flexibility is in the number of people employed, then redundancies are inevitably more likely to occur.' (Budget speech, 18 March 1986)

Shifting some of the burden of adjustment to short term conditions onto pay will help firms maintain a more stable labour force. A firm that does this can thus reconcile the need for financial flexibility, with demands for an internal strategy involving the competitive management of human investment, the raising of skills levels, and the retention of valuable employees.

What is required is that a visible indicator of the trading conditions which a firm faces be included in employees' contracts. Companies' profits can meet this need. Relating pay to profits is by no means new. For much of this century profit-sharing schemes have been used by a number of companies as means to increase the commitment of employees and to give them an incentive to be more productive. Tying a modest proportion of total remuneration to profits has been successfully achieved in many companies. In addition, since 1987 tax breaks have been available to United Kingdom companies operating approved forms of profit-related pay. It is important, if a firm is to achieve financial flexibility and retain personnel, that the *downside* of corporate performance is reflected in pay as well as the upside. Profit-related pay must not come to increase, ratchet-like, in an upwards-direction only. A growing body of evidence supports the view that profit-related pay can secure for companies both flexibility and retention.

Japan has been the source of many innovations in Western management techniques in recent years. Among the distinctive characteristics of companies there, is the long term employment relations which can be observed between employees and firms – a virtual lifetime employment contract. This makes for a remarkable degree of stability in employment within Japanese enterprises. This has helped companies develop highly-skilled workforces, able to produce goods of the very highest quality. Yet Japanese companies' ability to manage external uncertainty is entrenched in a flexible pay system which has a strong profit-related element. As a result pay fluctuates much more markedly than in typical Western organizations.

Closer to home, the experience of financial institutions in the City of London in the period surrounding the market deregulation (*Big Bang*) of October 1986 is instructive. In the run-up to deregulation City firms spent vast resources in attracting and engaging expert traders, analysts and sales staff, building teams ready to face the expected competitive onslaught. Salaries, while high, typically included a substantial bonus element which fluctuated with the profitability of the firm and individual's personal contribution to it. For some traders the variable portion of pay approached 80 per cent of initial total remuneration.

In the event Big Bang was followed by much less business in the City of London than was anticipated. Few trading floors were making much surplus, and the companies operating them were squeezed. Yet it remained uncertain whether the low volume levels were just a temporary phenomenon or would persist. City firms were forced to decide whether to lay-off many staff recruited only months before – at enormous cost in headhunters' fees and lump sum inducements, so-called *Golden Hellos* – or to wait to see whether the downturn would persist.

The fact that much of pay was bonus-related allowed the firms to bear much of the contraction in business. It increased the ability of firms to withstand delaying redundancies until it became clear that the downturn in volume was not a short term aberration.

It is certain that were City salaries fixed, lay-offs would have been forced on firms far quicker than was in fact the case. When substantial redundancies did take place in 1989, firms could be confident that they were not shortsightedly dropping valuable personnel.

The Business Performance Group studied the British financial services sector, the sector of the economy where profit-related pay is the most common and long-established. Firms investigated in the Business Performance Group survey employed in total over 225,000 people in Britain, and the analysis was of a twenty year period ending in 1987. This new evidence demonstrated that the introduction of a profit-related pay scheme by a company was typically associated with a significant reduction in the variability of employment over subsequent years. The study pinpointed in particular the role of the variability of pay in accounting for this greater stability: both the variability of basic pay, and the presence of profit-related pay, were instrumental in promoting a more stable level of employment over time, even having allowed for variations in the business and economic climate (Clark, 1992).

For a company considering introducing profit-related pay as part of an internal strategy to marry cost flexibility to the development of human capital, evidence available may not be conclusive. The experience of Japanese companies, for example, is tempered by an awareness that their arrangements with their employees have a very specific cultural and institutional underpinning. It is likely that a move to profit-related pay for these internal strategic reasons will be advantageous in some circumstances and unworkable in others.

Two apparent stumbling blocks are especially large. The first, how to introduce profit-related pay in the first instance; the second, how to maintain it in operation.

The first of these points brings into question what schemes can be said to fall under the heading, *Profit-Related Pay*: it will be an unusual workforce which will accept without compensation a step increase in income risk. This need not be a fatal objection to the introduction of profit-related pay as a medium term strategic objective, introduced sensitively as with other strategic initiatives. In such circumstances profit-related pay may be brought in initially as a bonus in addition to basic pay. But under the maxim, 'you get what you pay for', if the whole package is communicated to the workforce and potential recruits, the superior pay being offered can be expected to allow the firm to build up, over time, a superior workforce, whose performance makes the total package approximate to a market wage for such a group of people. Effective communication therefore becomes vital. In addition tax incentives have allowed many firms to make the introduction of a profit-related component to pay coincide with a government-sponsored increase in total pay.

Maintaining a profit-related programme over the years involves ensuring that employees do not become too disaffected during lean spells, affecting productivity and quitting rates. Some reassurance may be drawn from the fact that when the profit-related component is low, labour market conditions external to the firm are likely to be slack with other companies' demand for labour low. It would nevertheless be important to communicate the real benefits of flexible pay: greater security of employment (which in the long term can be expected to be established through reputation) and greater scope for training and development. Both of these factors can be important sources of competitive differentiation between firms in times of tight labour market conditions. We know that most workers themselves wish to undergo training, which will make them more productive, and so generally improve their earnings, and which will contribute to their personal development.

While the benefits of profit-related pay are real and are genuinely attainable, companies contemplating its introduction must take care to assess its suitability for their particular workforce. Human behaviour is rarely wholly calculating and rational, and sometimes and in some places the values and mores of the workforce will cause a move to more flexible pay to be damaging if introduced insensitively or, sometimes, at all. Businesses such as financial services may be seen to be associated with an individualism and flexibility among staff which makes an innovation such as flexible pay less contentious.

Similarly some types of employee may be more amenable than others: salesforces typically are used to more variable pay through the role of commission. Companies which have maintained very traditional industrial relations practices may find that its workforce cannot countenance such a change, in contrast to the more open policy agenda of greenfields sites establishments. Attention must therefore be paid to the circumstances in which the pay system would operate.

This is not to say that the circumstances cannot be deliberately changed. There is no doubt that company policies can change employees' behaviour and, with that, their conceptions of what is acceptable. As Nobel Laureate Sir James Meade said of employee share ownership, 'it may not be a waste of time to make... changes which are somewhat out of harmony with present attitudes, but may well in time help to mould these attitudes in the desired direction.' (Meade, 1989, p.2)

Profit-related pay may be a valuable tool in the *internal strategies* which companies are increasingly pursuing. In the medium term it may be a means to combine flexibility with effective management of human capital. In the longer term it can enhance further the opportunities to see and use employees as valuable assets.

13
Profit-Related Pay: The Implications for the Economy

Christopher Huhne

Who benefits when companies modify their compensation systems to include profit-sharing or employee share ownership? Certainly the employees gain, but so do the shareholders.

In recent years the evidence has been mounting that innovative schemes for remuneration are no bar to superior profitability. For example, Wallace Bell and Hanson (1987), compared the performance of companies with and without profit-sharing between 1977 and 1985. The average return on equity was 25.1 per cent for the 113 profit-sharing companies, and 19.9 per cent for the 301 non-profit sharing companies. In other words, profit sharers earned 5.2 per cent more on their shareholders' funds each year. Not surprisingly, profit sharers also did better in terms of earnings per share, return on sales, annual growth in sales and equity, and so on. The authors concluded that 'the economic performance of profit-sharing companies taken as a group was superior by a significant degree to that of non-profit sharers as a group in terms of profitability, growth and investor returns.'

Of course, the profit-sharing companies may have been earning above average profits before they introduced profit-sharing . Profit-sharing could be the result of high profitability, rather than its cause. However, it seems most likely (for reasons to be discussed below), that profit-sharing fosters good performance. Another study, conducted by Peat Marwick McLintock for the Department of Employment, interviewed in-depth 20 companies which had a significant degree of employee share ownership. Not one felt that the introduction of employee shareholding had had negative consequences. Most thought the impact was positive. Respondents had no doubt about what was causing what.

What happens when companies move away from fixed pay and add elements related to performance, either shares or cash profits? The macro-economic consequences essentially result from an aggregation of the consequences for individual firms, so let us start there. Does the change improve the performance of the company in an economic sense, by improving output per unit of input?

The old system of fixed pay is, symbolically, just like any other transaction in the market. You negotiate a price, you pay, you receive the goods. The transaction may be friendly, but it is basically a market exchange, involving little more than the cash nexus. With profit-sharing, an element of employees' pay varies in line with the payments to the owners of the company, and this link dilutes the implicitly adversarial nature of the market bargain. The relationship becomes (at least in part) implicitly co-operative. And when people become, in however small a way, *partners* rather than employees, internal conflicts in the organization are likely to be reduced. Their competitive energies will be directed to the real competition – the firms in the same market – rather than fellow workers or bosses. This does not mean that the company as a whole will become more herbivore, less competitive, in its external behaviour. Just as individuals readily assume different roles in different circumstances, firms can be co-operative internally and ruthless externally – against their competitors (see chapter 14).

A second economic consequence of a move toward profit related pay relates to risk-sharing. When employees' remuneration varies with the profits of the business, they assume some of the risk which is otherwise borne entirely by the owners of the enterprise. In some years, employees' total compensation will be relatively high (compared with the fixed pay received by their counterparts in other companies), in others relatively low. (This is one reason why profit-sharing will tend to become more popular as living standards rise; once their basic needs are met, people are more willing to have their next increment of income come from a more risky source.)

The economic consequences of this variability can be crucial. Ordinarily, when a company's financial performance declines – whether because its markets are depressed or because interest rates have unexpectedly doubled – it may need to shed labour in order to control its costs. The profit-sharing company, on the other hand, finds that its pay bill drops automatically in hard times (because there is less, or no, profit to share with employees). In this respect, the profit-related pay company may be better able to withstand a recession than the orthodox company: with less need to lay people off, it is less likely to find its long term strategy undermined by turbulence. The economy as a whole benefits because a decline in demand for products will have a less adverse impact on unemployment. Counter-inflationary policy would be less painful because prices and costs would tend to respond more quickly to a slow down in product markets (see chapter 12).

Employees who work in a profit-sharing enterprise face a second source of risk, namely the competence of the management. The returns of the business will depend on the soundness of managers' decisions as well as on environmental conditions. It appears, however, that companies which adopt profit-sharing schemes tend to be relatively well-managed since the implementation of profit-related pay changes the relationship between employees and managers in a way that improves managers' performance.

This is the third great advantage of unorthodox pay systems: it legitimises and makes positive the discontent which usually festers underneath the surface in any company. There are many possible ways of soliciting constructive criticism from employees, from suggestion boxes to quality circles (see chapter 9). However, profit-sharing will be particularly effective, because it gives employees an immediate, legitimate interest in improving the company's performance. Sir Peter Thompson of the National Freight Corporation remarked that it was a shock to his management team when they found themselves suddenly faced with a great many exceptionally well-informed shareholders bristling with ideas for improving the company's performance. Fortunately, the National Freight Corporation managers were big enough and brave enough to turn that newly legitimised interest to spectacularly good use (for a discussion of the National Freight Consortium see Bradley and Nejad, 1989).

I can testify to the same effect from my own experience as business editor of *The Independent* and the *Independent on Su.iday*. Although every employee of Newspaper Publishing plc, the company which owns the *Independent* and the *Independent on Sunday*, has shares or options and we also introduced profit-related pay as well. It is no accident that we have the lowest cost structure in the quality newspaper market despite relatively high pay. Quite serious cost-saving measures have been made much easier than they would have been in any other organization with which I have been involved – including the *Guardian, Manchester Evening News*, *The Economist* and the *Liverpool Daily Post and Echo* – and there is a widespread corporate culture of revenue-maximization and cost-minimization. In economic terms, these advantages make the company much more effective than most of its rivals.

Unorthodox pay systems have also been argued to have favourable consequences for employment, although I personally am not entirely convinced. This was the view advanced by Martin Weitzman, a brilliant American economist whose book *The Share Economy* inspired Mr Nigel Lawson, then Chancellor of the Exchequer, to offer tax incentives for profit-related pay in the 1987 budget. In principle, Weitzman noted, firms should go on hiring more people until the extra cost of hiring the next employee exactly equals the extra revenue that employee is likely to bring in. In other words, output will expand to the point at which marginal costs are equal to marginal revenue, in economists' jargon. A profit-sharing economy, Weitzman added, would build in a dynamic of expansion, because companies' marginal cost – the basic pay element in the total remuneration package – is actually lower when part of pay is profit-related. Low basic pay plus profit-sharing will keep the economy heading towards full employment because firms will constantly be hiring more workers whose marginal product exceeds their marginal cost.

One suspects, however, that employers would soon come to think of cost as meaning some smoothed average of profit-related pay. Moreover, they might begin to regard profit-related pay as an element in employees' remuneration that must be offset by an above average rise in basic pay if profits fall short. If that view were to gain ground, it could erode the advantages of profit-related pay in protecting a company against recession.

Some might argue that profit-related pay could discourage firms from making new investments in capital equipment, since the advantages of those investments would accrue partly to the workforce rather than the shareholders. I do not find this objection persuasive, because investment decisions are influenced by so many other factors.

In addition to their inherent economic effects, profit-related pay and employee share ownership offer certain tax advantages. Because the Treasury believes that both companies and society as a whole can benefit from profit-related pay, it allows companies to distribute profit related pay tax free, up to a limit of 10 per cent of salary or £6,000, whichever is higher. In other words, both employer and employee can enrich themselves at the Inland Revenue's expense. Profit-related pay has a further non-economic advantage (in the eyes of some): the potential to act as a *poison pill* that makes a company less attractive for take-over. Whether that is good or bad economically is entirely another debate.

What then can we conclude about profit-related pay? Various *hard* justifications have been proposed in recent years, related to dynamic employment gains and protection against recession. These advantages, however, seem to be to be more open to doubt, and to erosion over time, than the benefits more traditionally claimed, involving improved motivation and management. Although the *soft* arguments may sound woolly and mushy, in reality they carry considerable force.

At first glance it may appear that profit-sharing would reduce the returns to shareholders. Both theory and empirical evidence suggest, however, that this is not a zero sum game. Profit-related pay changes the relationships within companies in ways which make them more co-operative and more efficient economic units. As a result, shareholders will make more profits by sharing them with employees.

14
Competitive Success through Participation: The John Lewis Partnership

Simon Taylor

Introduction

The John Lewis Partnership is one of the United Kingdom's most famous retailers, with a reputation among customers and competitors for quality and success. This success is of particular interest because the John Lewis Partnership has been owned entirely by its workforce (known collectively as the *partners*) since 1929. All undistributed profits are allocated to the partners, in proportion to their salaries. Moreover, the John Lewis Partnership embodies a set of business and organization principles which are rooted in a particular conception of industrial democracy and participation.

British experience with cooperatives and with participation has not always been a happy one, at least judged from the perspective of business. The *Benn cooperatives* of the 1970s were poor advertisements for the supposed benefits to a company of greater employee participation[1]. Moreover, conventional economics and management thinking suggests that a firm like the John Lewis Partnership would be a business disaster, for two reasons. First, it has no capital market discipline, since it has little debt and cannot be taken over if it performs poorly (all shares are held by the trust on behalf of the partners). Second, employee involvement in decision making has often been argued to lead to short-termism, as current workers seek to run down the capital and borrow, eating up the longer term value of the firm.

Yet, judged by conventional financial accounting criteria, the John Lewis Partnership is a marked success, scoring high on productivity, profitability and growth both in the department stores and on the supermarkets side (Waitrose Limited). Nor is there any evidence of short-termism or excessively high bonus payouts. In fact, the story of the John Lewis Partnership illustrates the value of attention to the human side of the business. We will consider the ways in which the Partnership model can contribute to the business solutions of the 1990s.

The John Lewis Partnership and its competitors

As a private company with very little securitized debt, the John Lewis Partnership has not been given much attention by the capital markets and does not feature in retail sector rankings. However, a detailed study of the company in relation to leading supermarkets and stores shows that the Partnership would do very well, judged by the conventional reporting criteria. In terms of profitability, productivity and growth, the John Lewis Partnership scores at the top of the range, along with market leaders such as Marks and Spencer, Sainsbury and Tesco.

Table 14.1 Compound growth of productivity data* – 1970-89

	JLP	M&S	Sainsbury	Tesco
Turnover/fixed assets	2.1	0.3	-4.7	-3.1
Turnover/labour	14.4	13.2	13.6	12.8
Full time employment	2.9	0.7	3.7	5.7
Part time employment	3.4	7.1	7.4	4.8

Fixed assets and turnover quoted in nominal terms; labour measured by full time equivalent employment.

As table 14.1 shows, the John Lewis Partnership has achieved the highest growth of productivity of both capital and labour, as measured by the compound growth rate of fixed assets and full time labour equivalent to turnover. Interestingly, the John Lewis Partnership has made much greater use of full-time workers than other leading retail firms, which have followed a general trend towards greater part-time working.

A fuller exposition and details of concepts and measurement are given in Bradley *et al* (1990). Bradley and Taylor (1992) shows that the John Lewis Partnership scores highly on return on capital, liquidity and gearing, and that the share of earnings distributed as the partnership bonus is small in comparison with the dividend payouts of conventional firms. In sum, the John Lewis Partnership is financially sound and would command a very strong share price, were it a quoted company.

Furthermore, the financial success is backed by a very high reputation among its competitors, who all acknowledge the consistently high standards set by the Partnership.

How has this company managed to achieve commercial success, saddled with an apparently unhelpful structure and lacking the takeover discipline that is usually seen as necessary to discipline managers? To answer this question, we turn to the business ideas on which the firm is run, known as *Partnership Principles*.

Partnership Principles

The John Lewis Partnership is very much the creation of a single man, John Spedan Lewis, who set up the employee-owned trust in 1929 and instituted a system of representative participation in 1953. The Partnership is based on a constitution designed by Lewis, which continues to form the basis of management strategy and decision-taking.

At the root of Spedan Lewis' beliefs about management and work were his views on the relations between labour and capital. The central proposition is that there should be an upper bound to the amount that owners of capital can properly expect as a reward for assuming risk. This belief was built upon Lewis' own experience of deriving significant amounts of profit from the company, in some years more than the total wage bill, in exchange for bearing little if any risk. He found it unfair that capital should have an open-ended right to receive excess or *windfall* profits while unskilled workers' pay was relatively fixed, even in periods of great profitability. Lewis describes the relation as one of 'dishonest' broking (Lewis, 1954, p. 165). The legal open-ended right of capital owners to the residual profits Lewis termed the 'equity principle', which he decisively rejected.

Lewis' opposition to the equity principle as the basis for an economic order became the starting point for a theory of how to motivate staff and generate a more *efficient* business, as well as a fairer one. The aims of the Partnership included raising the material rewards to partners, which would require productivity increases. Fairness, perhaps more than other features of the John Lewis Partnership, helped to achieve these gains. But Lewis' enthusiasm went further; his conception of sharing apparently extended to the sheer enjoyment of running and being involved in a business venture[2].

Fairness as a business principle therefore arose from both *financial* and *ethical* motives. In the 1990s, it has become a commonplace of the business world that treating staff with a sense of justice should lead to gains in productivity and competitive advantage. This is notably true of the retail sector (Taylor, 1989, Ch. 12). In this respect, as in many others, Lewis was ahead of his time.

Although Lewis' initial motivation for his reforms was ethical, he was a hard-headed businessman. He criticised the socialist claim, that partnership does not go far enough, by arguing that without some material inducement most people will not give the full effort of which they are capable, and that the 'system of partnership is simply a way of recognising and accepting these facts of human nature without going needlessly far in the direction of inequality.' (Lewis, 1954, p. 13)

Lewis' beliefs about how best to run a business were heavily influenced by the general political philosophy sketched above. In addition he emphasized a number of other principles on which to maximise motivation and efficiency. These ideas seem to have been derived largely from experience rather than doctrine.

First, Lewis cited *security of employment*, and general humanity, as critical factors in determining recruitment and retention of good staff. High pay may be effective in attracting new employees, but will not necessarily persuade them to remain in an unpleasant work environment. (Lewis cites the high turnover of staff at Henry Ford's plants as an example.) Hence, especially if costs of quits are an important element in the firm's operations, it will want to provide job security as well as a humane working environment.

Second, a *sense of justice* was seen as crucial to effective team-work performance. Lewis appealed to management to be hard-headedly fair. He acknowledged that justice alone is not a panacea: there will still be problems and times which may be *grim* (Lewis, 1954, p. 163). Lewis believes in the intelligent pursuit of happiness as a conscious management goal. Justice is particularly important to this. In Lewis' view, the most brazen injustice was introduced by the asymmetry of rewards for risk. Shocks to the business would undoubtedly occur, he recognised; what mattered was the manner in which they were propagated, especially as between workers and shareholders.

Thirdly, Lewis stresses the need for *incentives*, including material rewards. However, he seems to regard the need to provide appropriate incentives primarily as a constraint on the more general ambition of first setting, and then progressively raising, the minimum wage. His book *Partnership For All* evinces some confusion, or at least some inconsistency, on this issue. At one point he suggested that not only are workers well-paid because they are able, but quite plausibly the converse is true also (Lewis, 1954, p. 167). He does not explore the implications of this principle for pay determination.[3] Lewis may have been appealing indirectly for a basic and *decent* minimum wage, but this is not very convincing in the context of his main view of incentives. He was apparently happy to pay people high salaries if it was necessary and if they performed well, so long as the income was a reward for work, not a return to financial wealth.

Lewis inherited from his father a devotion to the principle of *customer service*, although the elder Lewis restricted his notion of service to the range and quality of goods rather than the role of the staff in providing that service. The current chairman and former chairman of the John Lewis Partnership both believe that the Partnership Principles, aside from any other merits, increase the level of customer service. As current chairman, Peter Lewis, puts it:

> 'It does work particularly well in retailing. It encourages smiling faces across the counter.'[4]

In conversation, it appears that there is a widespread perception among staff at the John Lewis Partnership that the level of customer service is better than elsewhere and that this is one aspect of their commercial success. Peter Lewis' predecessor, Sir Bernard Miller, explains:

> '...the retail trade is fertile ground for the Partnership system because in retailing, whatever organization you've got, the man or woman behind the counter is the business to the customer on the other side of the counter... [W]hatever he or she does is, in the eyes of the customer, what the business is doing.'[5]

This potential is then linked to the incentives that the Partnership system offers to individual partners:

> 'If you can get in individuals a sense that they're working for themselves and they're behaving as a small shopkeeper would behave if his own business was at stake, then of course you've got a plus that really scores, and I think this is why it's been so successful in the retail trade.'[6]

Sir Bernard goes on to suggest that the system works well in the non-retail areas of the John Lewis Partnership also, and that there is no reason in principle that it should not be applied in any business.

Partnership institutions

The conception of employee rights in the John Lewis Partnership hinges on the *right to be represented*.[7] This can mean the right to voice discontent, without any direct participation in power, or it can mean the right to vote for or otherwise influence the executive.

This right is made effective by the management's general willingness to take notice of what the workers' representatives have to say, as they are constitutionally obliged to do, backed by a strong sense of corporate culture that management *should* listen.

Perhaps the most striking aspect of the accountability system at the John Lewis Partnership is that the chairman (appointed by his predecessor) can be voted out of his position by the elected representatives. This has never happened, but the knowledge that it could helps keep the chairman on his toes, and enhances the authority of senior management.

Partners elect representatives to serve on the Central Council, which has two related functions. First, it raises issues (which may have come direct from partners at a shop floor level) for formal but open discussion with senior management. Second, the Council has certain, largely negative, powers, such as the right to veto amendments to the constitution;[8] in addition it plays a role in electing trustees and members of the Central Board.

It would be unreasonable to expect a large representative body such as the Council to take part directly in executive decision making; in practice its leverage over the Board is apparently rather less than, say, that of Parliament over the cabinet. The Council appointees to the Board have the right to demand that certain issues be brought to the Council for discussion, including major lay-offs or changes in the capital structure, but on the whole the power of the Council lies in simply raising issues and confronting management on them.

These representative structures, which can confront management, air grievances or simply ask questions, are complemented by two-way flows of information in the John Lewis Partnership's internal publications. This combination appears to make for a credible system of accountability. This is one of the most distinctive features of the John Lewis Partnership, although it is not quite what most observers would describe as industrial democracy. However, employee representation and two-way flows of information are not incompatible. Within certain limits, the John Lewis Partnership approach may be compatible with a more conventional ownership structure.

Reasons for the John Lewis Partnership's success

The Partnership appears to have struck a highly efficient balance between the needs of an effective business and the mechanisms for motivating the workforce. From the first, the idea of giving workers a greater say in the business, both financially and in terms of representation, was rooted in the realities of running a business. No system can be viable if it does not allow the basic business to thrive and prosper. Many attempts at participation and cooperation have failed precisely because they overemphasise ideology and pay too little attention to the need to sell a product.

The system of Partnership Principles delivers lower staff turnover and a powerful management authority (Bradley *et al.*, 1990; Flanders *et al.*, 1968). It therefore provides a far better environment for training and improved customer service. In particular, product knowledge is a major component of customer service, and this is an area in which the John Lewis Partnership traditionally excels.

While it is impossible to infer precisely how far the Partnership system translates into business success, the evidence is highly encouraging for the Lewis line. The fact that other retailing firms are moving increasingly in the same direction as the John Lewis Partnership suggests that they believe its model will be conducive to business success in the 1990s. For example, many retailers now have profit-sharing schemes, and many are putting greater emphasis on customer service. More generally, retailing companies are taking the human side of their business much more seriously. Traditionally, most of the retail sector has neglected training and relied on a steady stream of flexible and cheap young workers. This approach is now becoming unrealistic, given adverse demographic trends and the increasing sophistication of the tasks that retail staff must perform.

The result is that retail competitive strategy is shifting in the direction of competing through people, both at the level of customer service on the shop floor, and in terms of high quality managers who are familiar with complex distribution and buying systems.[9]

The model of the new retailing firm, then, is looking more and more like the John Lewis Partnership: offering financial participation, greater emphasis on training and career development, and aiming for a stable and well-motivated workforce. It remains to be seen how far these elements can be achieved in the context of a conventional firm ownership and control structure.

Lessons for the 1990s

The John Lewis Partnership has been commercially successful because it has addressed certain business challenges that reflect the changing economic structure of the late twentieth century. These include:

1)   The focus on *services*, rather than goods.

2)   The use of new *technology*.

3)   The increasing *flexibility* of use of labour.

4)   The *competition for the customer's time*, as an indirect form of leisure activity.

5) And, embracing all of these characteristics, the emphasis on
    customer service.

Many firms, across the range of manufacturing as well as traditional
service sectors, face these same issues. The experience of the John
Lewis Partnership suggests that a great deal can be achieved by
concentrating managers' attention on the human side of the business.
By contrast, the traditional view of competitive strategy tends to place
human issues very low down the list. By the time it becomes clear that
business is being lost because of personnel-related difficulties, it may be
too late to do much about it.

Lewis saw that a sense of justice, backed by substantial material
incentives, is a good starting point for any shift in emphasis towards
service and greater employee flexibility and creativity. This fundamental insight has a wide resonance across businesses in the early 1990s.
There is an interesting parallel with large Japanese firms, which gain a
similar degree of collective commitment to the company goals.

Conclusion

The unexpected success of the John Lewis Partnership is evidence that
taking people seriously and placing them at the heart of the business
strategy can deliver consistent competitive advantage. The practices
adopted by the John Lewis Partnership are mutually reinforcing and
permit greater investment in training and a smooth employee relations
climate.

A replication of the John Lewis Partnership experiment may not be a
realistic options for most firms. But businesses interested in customer
service and training – in short those firms which take the people side of
the business seriously – can learn a great deal from the success of the
John Lewis Partnership.

15

Human Resources as Social Capital

Richard Caruso

The concept of *social capital*

Since the industrial revolution, finance capital has been a crucial element in firms' efforts to remain competitive. Mass production technologies required heavy investment in plant and equipment, but relatively little skill on the part of workers. Over time, however, as businesses evolved and became more complex, new flexible, cross-application technologies were introduced into the work place. This development, together with increased international competition and changes in the composition of the workforce, made expert individuals more important to the firm. Today such employees constitute a larger portion of the workforce, and for many firms they represent the assets and social capital necessary for competitive survival. Increasingly, the social capital of many contemporary firms may be as important as their finance capital.

Social capital and finance capital

The way a firm acquires and develops finance capital depends on both its needs and its ability to satisfy the criteria of the finance capital market. In acquiring finance capital, a firm may choose between *equity* or *debt*, or a combination of the two. At the same time, the market may deny the firm either or both of these sources of funds, depending on the nature of the firm, its business prospects, and conditions in the financial markets. Over time, businesses have evolved standardised ways of reporting on both kinds of finance capital.

From an accounting and finance perspective, equity capital is often viewed as providing the firm's basic underlying strength or substance, which is often associated with its core strength or competitive ability. Through their business activities, companies either develop their equity capital (by earning a profit), or lose it (by incurring a loss). Equity is also reduced through the payment of dividends or other distributions. Debt financing is classified as a liability and is generally viewed as a financial burden on a firm (although it also enables the enterprise to pursue its business objectives).

One can also distinguish between social equity capital – an organization's core of expertise – and a debt form of social capital. In practice, expert employees are not all equally effective in furthering organizational goals. We may say that the organization's social debt capital consists of expert employees who contribute to organizational objectives, but at a higher cost than that of social equity capital. The higher cost of social debt capital may reflect (i) a lower commitment to the organization on the part of expert employees, resulting in lower production or higher turnover; (ii) job assignments that require greater skills than the expert employee has to offer; (iii) insufficient training; (iv) poor communications; and (v) an asymmetry between expert employees' career objectives and organizational goals. To the extent these factors increase a firm's social debt capital, they decrease the value of its social equity capital.

Depending on the nature of the business, the less effective (or higher cost) group may make the firm less competitive, less profitable, or both. But just as debt financing may be appropriate in some circumstances, debt social capital is not inherently a bad thing. In certain businesses, the less effective (higher cost) group of employees may help make the company more competitive and more profitable in the long run. Although firms' social capital is a matter of some interest to their stakeholders, it has not been the subject of formal reporting. Accountants do not classify or measure an organization's social capital, the associated costs, or the suggested distinction between social equity and debt capital in their certified financial statements.

Acquisition of finance and social capital

Organizations acquire finance capital largely on the strength of their financial statements, balance sheet and business prospects. A variety of tools have been developed, such as ratio analysis, financial projections and profitability analysis, to assess a firm's optimum mix of equity and debt financing. (Getting the mix right is considered to have some influence on financial profitability, and in turn on the value of the firm's shares (equity).) Assuming both equity and debt finance are readily available, the company would ordinarily choose between the two on the basis of relative cost.

In a circular logic, companies attempt to become more attractive to providers of both types of finance by earning a profit on their business activity. As a result, they develop their own finance equity capital, which presumably lowers the cost of future financing, enabling them to earn even larger profits. For many contemporary companies, however, social capital is an equally important determinant of profitability and economic competitiveness. Stakeholders of such firms ought to be concerned with a variety of questions that are ignored in conventional, financially oriented accounting statements. For example:

> How does a company acquire its social capital? How much social capital should a company have?
> How much has it already?
> What is an appropriate mix of debt and equity in social debt capital?
> Should a firm attempt to become more attractive to the social capital market? If so, how?
> Can efforts to improve current employees' career satisfaction in the firm make it easier to acquire further attractive social capital?

Many business organizations initially acquire much of their social capital by recruiting talented graduates from educational institutions. One goal of the interview process may be to select individuals whose goals and objectives appear to be compatible with those of the organization. Conceivably, such a focus on the potential to develop a shared vision among organization members may be the single most important step in acquiring social capital. Once new recruits join the organization, however, the challenge becomes the development of the social capital that they represent, a process that depends on both the firm's specific needs and the particular objectives of the individual employees.

Development of finance and social capital and its classification into debt and equity

When a firm acquires finance capital, it knows the amount at the outset. With social capital, by contrast, the number of new recruits can be tallied immediately, but their value to the organization may be revealed only through the development process (eg, individual career development for the benefit of the firm). The classification between equity and debt also may not be clear until development.

Educational institutions create technical or knowledge experts, by teaching skills to individuals; they pay little attention to the ways in which such knowledge is employed in an organization. Individual career development, on the other hand, may be largely a matter of communicating and applying expertise, rather than knowledge *per se*. From the firm's perspective, it is the ability of employees to apply their knowledge that determines the value of their social capital.

To develop their social capital, firms may attempt to influence employees' techniques of applying expertise and knowledge, and their communication ability, and may attempt to synthesize organizational goals with individual career objectives. For example, career development schemes might direct employees' energies and influence their career goals towards the pursuit of a vision shared by both the individual and the firm. This development process helps to determine the classification of individuals as social equity capital or social debt capital.

Careful planning may be needed to ensure optimal development of the firm's social capital, and an appropriate division between equity and debt. If there is too much in the equity category, talented, aspiring new individuals may not be able to pursue their career objectives within the company and may therefore leave the firm. The result would be a reduction of the flow of new ideas and creative thinking brought into the social equity category by such individuals, with possibly adverse effects on the evolution of the firm's competitive strategy and direction.

Because debt social capital can play a constructive role, firms do not necessarily attempt to develop all their acquired social capital into social equity capital. If a steady supply of talented new recruits is available, a firm may try to increase its *social capital leverage* by acquiring, year after year, the best available new social capital from the marketplace. Its expectation may be that many of the new recruits will initially develop careers within the organization, and then voluntarily leave for perceived better opportunities. Such a firm may have determined that, in the long run, the cost of the best new social capital may be less than the cost of keeping older developed social capital. This pattern may be more characteristic of professional firms than of manufacturing organizations.

Many firms recruit a large number of entry level expert personnel in order to be able to service clients, or to staff functions. They often expect that a sizeable portion of the new recruits will leave voluntarily after some period of time. Similarly, individuals may join a firm because they believe it is a good place to start a career, but without an expectation that they will remain there indefinitely. Each successive wave of new recruits is routinely replaced with another (though the firm may attempt to retain the best of each cohort).

Such a strategy may work well for the firm so long as it can draw on a continuous supply of new recruits. In effect, the core base of expert individuals, such as the partners of a law firm or the senior engineers of a manufacturing firm, leverage off a readily available market supply of new blood. The company is willing to bear the higher short run cost of social debt capital (which is relatively flexible), rather than risk developing too much longer term, inelastic social equity capital. The balance between debt and equity forms of social capital will vary with the market supply of new expert individuals (perhaps the single most important determinant of a firm's social capital strategy), the attractiveness of a firm's social capital environment, its need to retain such individuals, and the nature of its business.

In planning a social capital strategy, it is important to remember that individuals may want to decide for themselves whether they belong in the debt or the equity category. If a compatible relationship is to develop, either the firm or the individual may have to change. A continual mismatch between individual objectives and organizational goals is not a good sign.

A further complication is that social capital classifications may shift during the time an individual employee remains with the firm. A change from debt to equity (or *vice versa*) might reflect an increase (or decrease) in mutual commitment and individual motivation, or a growing consonance (or inconsistency) between the career goals of the individual and the aims of the organization.

Dividends and interest with respect to finance and social capital

Many organizations pay a periodic cash dividend on finance equity capital, make distributions of finance equity capital and pay interest on finance debt capital. The amount and timing of these payments generally depends on the success of the firm's recent business activity and on its expected need for financial capital in the near future. Similarly, firms pay a sort of dividend to their social equity capital, comprising both higher monetary compensation (perhaps including profit sharing or equity participation as well as periodic pay) and non-monetary rewards, such as greater commitment to such employees, opportunities for an interesting and challenging job, and career development. Interest on a firm's social debt capital characteristically takes the form of monetary rewards rather than organizational commitment or employment security.

Distributions of social capital

Social capital may be dispersed by the firm, when it reduces staff.

Sometimes, however, employees leave of their own accord, thereby diminishing the firm's social capital. Whether they have left voluntarily or involuntarily, former employees can continue to influence the nature and cost of a firm's social capital; what they say to others about their experience in the organization may make it easier (or more difficult) to attract new recruits (or fresh infusions of financial capital). Former employees may also influence the firm's potential profitability by recommending it (or not) to potential customers.

Social capital and strategic planning

A first step in planning for the acquisition, development, and distribution of social capital is to assess the firm's own attributes. For instance, a high value-added service sector firm may be a particularly good place to start but not necessarily the best place to develop a career. Its employees might find better specialised career opportunities elsewhere. Once they have left the firm, expert individuals may contribute to its favourable reputation if they feel it has significantly influenced their own career success. To this end, some business organizations sponsor alumni association meetings, bring ex-employees together to reflect and discuss a shared experience or a commonality of interest. Such activities may be considered part of the firm's social capital strategic plan.

When firms consciously turn over a large percentage of their newly acquired employees, this could be seen as a form of leveraging. This pattern – social equity capital leveraging off a continual supply of social debt capital – may have both positive and negative consequences for a firm. Its cost will depend on: (i) whether it is measured on a short or long term basis; (ii) the supply of social capital; (iii) the ability of the firm to attract new social capital; (iv) the nature of the firm; (v) the prospects for its business; and, perhaps more important, (vi) the career success or failure of employees who leave and those who stay.

If employees (past and present) tend to see this pattern of leveraging as exploitative, the firm may develop an unfavourable reputation, making it more difficult to acquire and develop new social capital in the future. When individuals approve of the company's approach to social capital, on the other hand, it may gain a reputation for making positive contributions to career development.

This view suggests that former employees represent a means for a firm to enhance its social capital, because they are a valuable source of employment recommendations and business referrals. However, this approach can create problems for a firm that needs a particular type of scarce social capital, especially if individuals with that expertise disapprove of the leveraging activity. Such a firm may need to work on schemes to retain all the social capital it can get at whatever realistic competitive costs it takes.

The ability of social capital to get up and walk away from the firm can create real difficulties. Companies have tried in a variety of ways to ensure that they do not lose valued employees. There is no single social capital strategy that is universally effective. National culture, the competitive marketplace and the nature of a firm and its business all make a difference. An approach that works in one country or in one firm may not work in another. Organizations unable to lock up or otherwise physically secure their social capital may need to create and maintain an organizational culture that attracts the best experts and encourages them to stay and develop their careers within the company.

Table 15.1 Finance and social capital: A comparison

	Financial capital	Social capital
Acquisition	Public and private offerings of equity and debt issues	Recruitment of expert employees
Development process	Earn a profit from business operations and increase retained earnings; incur and pay off debt	Training, socialize employees into the organization, synthesizing individual career objectives with organizational goals
Timing and nature of equity/debt category	Fixes upon acquisition and does not change over time	Determined through the development process and thereafter may change over time
Forms of dividend/interest distribution	Cash and cash equivalent	Cash and cash equivalent, plus non-monetary distributions
Forms of capital distribution	Voluntary cash and cash equivalent	Voluntary and involuntary non-monetary distributions
Nature	Cash, or its equivalent, generally indistinguishable	Non-cash; distinguishable and generally unique

Summary discussion

Social capital – the expertise and knowledge of employees, and their willingness to use it in support of organizational objectives – is both similar and dissimilar to finance capital. Whereas all dollar bills or pound notes are functionally equivalent, social capital consists of distinguishable individual units. The value of individual expert employees changes over time, as they become increasingly skilled and application competent, develop their careers and either synthesize their career goals with the organization or grow apart from it. Table 15.1 briefly compares selected aspects of finance capital and social capital.

New recruits join an existing organizational environment that developed over a period of time. If they find it friendly, they may be more inclined to develop a career within that organization. If the environment seems hostile, new employees may (i) feel hostility to the very organization that recruited them; (ii) decide that the company's goals are inconsistent with their own career objectives; (iii) feel thwarted in their efforts to practice their expertise and develop their desired careers within the organization; (iv) leave prematurely; and (v) think and speak unfavourably about the organization to others. From developing its social capital, such an organization might find that its existing social capital is haemorrhaging and it is unable to replace it with new social capital. How does one measure the social capital of a business organization? These issues merit further research and currently constitutes a part of the research agenda of the LSE Business Performance Group.

Notes

Chapter 2: The human capital audit and business performance

1. Our sample was achieved by interviewing every fourth person on Showcase's payroll. We used a structured questionnaire which respondents completed themselves. The questionnaire contained some 200 discrete data points and the survey yielded a sample of 350. This represented a 99 per cent response rate. The survey data was supplemented with some thirty-five in-depth interviews with key people in the organization.

Chapter 3: Population ageing and employment policies

1. OECD, *Ageing Populations: the Social Policy Implications*, Paris 1988. The assumptions incorporated in these projections are: i) Fertility: will remain at its current level in each country until 1995, and will then converge towards a common replacement fertility rate of 2.1 by 2050, ii) Life Expectancy at Birth: will increase by two years for each sex between 1983 and 2030, and will then remain constant to 2050.
2. Author's calculations, based on: Department of Health and Social Security, *Population, Pension Costs and Pensioners' Incomes*, HMSO, London, 1984.

Chapter 4: Excellence in personnel management

1. These factors were in place in IBM UK Limited in 1989.
2. These factors applied to IBM UK's personnel department in 1989.

Chapter 5: Human capital flows and business efficiency

1. This relatively recent data is not reflected in chapter 8 whose authors maintain a more traditional view. Editor's note.
2. Only 8 per cent of all secondary school pupils were in comprehensive schools in 1965 when Antony Crosland accelerated the pace of comprehensivisation.
3. One possibility is the City: banks and other financial institutions are omitted from the *Times 1000* list and so are not reflected in the top fifty tables in 5.1 and 5.2. Yet the public school elite were already too heavily concentrated there for there to be much increase in their numbers, and today it seems unlikely to have offered them a safe refuge from competition. See eg David Bower, *Class of 86*, *Business*, November 1986.
4. In 1951, 62 per cent of pupils aged sixteen plus were in maintained schools, 9 per cent in direct grant schools and 30 per cent in independent schools (Halsey *et al* 1972, p. 12). This mirrors the proportions in table 5.1, 40 per cent of independent school boys then stayed on in the sixth form, but of course only a small portion in the state sector did. This is compatible with the view that those with education had an equal chance of sixth form education which was a virtual prerequisite for top jobs.
5. The precipitous decline of Cambridge merits further investigations; like any of our results it may be *noise* in our small sample.

Chapter 7: Mentoring and the development of social capital

1. In 1986, PA Associates, a consulting firm published a report based on a questionnaire survey of senior executives of organizations in eight countries. Their survey found that companies feel career development is important, and planned mentoring programmes were increasingly popular as a means to attempt to facilitate career development. Out of 381 organizations which responded, sixty-seven reported some form of mentoring scheme in use and an additional eighty-eight were thinking about introducing a mentoring scheme. However, given that the sample was 2000 which yielded a response rate of 19 per cent, inferences from these findings are inconclusive, but might be indicative of an increasing organizational interest in mentoring.
2. See eg: *Employment Policies: Looking to the Year 2000*, National Alliance of Business (1986); *The world in 1989 and onto the 1990's*, The Economist (1988). See also Fullerton (1985), Personick (1985), and Silverton and Lukasiewicz (1985).

3. This is not to suggest that a closed mentoring relationship cannot satisfy many mentoring functions. However in an organizational setting it may exist within a larger construct which is satisfying additional mentoring needs not addressed in such closed mentoring relationships.
4. A closed system view might have been more appropriate in pre-large organization craftsman-apprentice relationships where the apprentice-protege received from his craftsman-mentor many mentoring functions, ie training, challenging tasks, role model, now generally available to contemporary proteges through organizational systems.
5. Our sample comprised 134 proteges and fifty-four mentors, all of whom had completed at least one year's formal mentoring. The response rate was 100 per cent.

Chapter 8: Management development and career success

1. Trust status implies that the individual hospital will have greater discretion over its finances and organization but still remains part of the National Health Service.

Chapter 14: Competitive success through participation: The John Lewis Partnership

1. In the 1970s ailing firms were sometimes converted into cooperatives by their employees. This strategy of redundant employees buying their companies was supported by Tony Benn, Secretary of State for Industry. Three British cooperatives formed in this way received government support and became known as the *Benn cooperatives*.
2. Interview with the author, June 1988.
3. The idea was later identified by economists and called the efficiency wage principle. See Akerlof and Yellen, (1986).
4. Interview between author and Peter Lewis, June 1989.
5. Interview between author and Sir Bernard Miller, June 1988.
6. *ibid.*
7. See Bernard Miller's foreword to Flanders *et al.*, (1968).
8. It also has a number of standing committees.
9. Bradley and Taylor (1992) discuss the shift in retailing strategy in greater depth, based on interviews with chief executives and chairmen.

Bibliography

Ackoff, R (1967). 'Management Misinformation Systems', *Management Science*, Vol. 14, No. 4.

Acton Society Trust (1956). *Management Succession.*

Akerlof, G and Yellen, J (1986). *Efficiency Wage Models of the Labour Market*, Cambridge University Press, Cambridge.

Alleman, E (1982). *Mentoring Relationships in Organizations: Behaviors, Personality Characteristics and Interpersonal Perceptions*, Unpublished PhD Thesis, University of Akron.

Armstrong, P (1989). 'Limits and Possibilities for HRM in an Age of Management Accountancy.' In Storey, J (ed) *New Perspectives on Human Resource Management*, Routledge, London.

Beer, M, Spector, B, Lawrence, P, Mills, Q, and Walton, R (1984). *Managing Human Assets*, The Free Press, New York.

Boehm, B (1988). 'Understanding and Controlling Software Costs', *IEEE Trans., Software Engineering*, Vol. 14, No. 10.

Bottoms, L W (1982). *The Interrelationships Among Sex-role Orientations, Self Actualization, and Significant Issues of High Achieving, Executive Women*, Unpublished PhD Thesis, Georgia State University, Georgia.

Bradley, K and Hill, S (1983). 'After Japan: the Quality Circle Transplant and Productive Efficiency', *British Journal of Industrial Relations*, Vol. 21, No. 3.

Bradley, K and Hill, S (1987). 'Quality Circles and Managerial Interests,' *Industrial Relations*, Berkeley, California, Vol. 26, No. 1.

Bradley, K, Estrin, S and Taylor, S (1990). 'Employee Ownership and Company Performance' *Industrial Relations*, Berkeley, California, Vol. 29, No. 3.

Bradley, K and Nejad, A (1989). *Managing Owners: The National Freight Consortium in Perspective*, Cambridge University Press, Cambridge.

Bradley, K and Taylor, S (1992). *Business Performance in the Retail Sector*, Oxford University Press, Oxford.

Caruso, R E (1990). *An Examination of Organisational Mentoring: The Case of Motorola*, Unpublished PhD Thesis, London School of Economics, London.

Checkland, P (1981). *Systems Thinking, Systems Practice*, Wiley, Chichester.

Clark, G (1992). *The Effects of Profit-Sharing on the Banking Sector, Papers on Performance*, Business Performance Group, London School of Economics.

Clawson, J G (1979). *Superior-subordinate Relationship in Managerial Development*, Unpublished PhD Thesis, Harvard University, Cambridge, Massachussetts.

Collard, R and Dale, B (1989). 'Quality Circles,' in Sisson, K (Ed.), *Personnel Management in Britain*, Blackwell, Oxford.

Crewe, I (1989). 'Values: the Crusade that Failed' in Kavanagh, D and Seldon, A (Eds) *The Thatcher Effect*, Clarendon Press, Oxford.

Crosby, P (1980). *Quality is Free*, New American Library, New York.

Dakin, S and Hamilton, R (1985). 'The Development of General Managers', *Management Decision*, Vol. 23, No.4.

Dalton, G and Thompson, P (1986). *Novations*, Scott, Foresman and Company, Illinois.

Davies, J (1983). 'Evaluating Training,' In Guest, B and Kenny, T (Eds), *A Textbook of Techniques and Strategies in Personnel Management*, Institute of Personnel Management, London.

Deal, T E and Kennedy, A (1982). *Corporate Cultures*, Penguin Books, London.

Deming, W (1986). *Out of the Crisis*. Cambridge University Press, Cambridge.

Department of Health and Social Security (1984). *Population, Pension Costs and Pensioners' Incomes*, Her Majesty's Stationery Office (HMSO), London.

Dreyfus, H L and Dreyfus, S E (1986). *Mind over Machine*, Blackwell, Oxford.

Economist, The 'The World in 1989 and Onto the 1990s', *The Economist*, London.

Edwards, P (1987). *Managing the Factory: A Survey of General Managers*, Blackwell, Oxford.

Feigenbaum, E, McCorduck, P and Nii, P G (1988). *The Rise of the Expert Company*, Macmillan, London.

Flanders, A, Pomeranz, R and Woodward, J (1968). *Experiment in Industrial Democracy*, Faber, London.

Fullerton, H N, Jr. (1985). 'The 1995 Labor Force: BLS' Latest Projections', *Monthly Labor Review*,.

Gall, J (1988). *Systemantics*, General Systemantics Press, Ann Arbor, Minneapolis.

Goldsmith, Sir J (1985). *Counter-Culture*, Privately published.

Goldsmith, W and Ritchie, B (1987). *The New Elite: Britain's Top Executives*, Weidenfeld and Nicholson, London.

Guest, D (1990). 'Personnel Management: The End of Orthodoxy?', Paper presented to the *1990 British Universities Industrial Relations Assocation Conference*, Warwick.

Guillemard, A (1989). 'The Trend towards early Labour Force Withdrawals and the Reorganization of the Life-course: A Cross-national Analysis' in Johnson, P, Conrad, C and Thomson, D (Eds) *Workers versus Pensioners: Intergenerational Justice in an Ageing World*. Manchester University Press, Manchester.

Hall, D, de Bettignies, H and Amado-Fischgrund, G (1969). 'The European Business Elite', *European Business*, No. 23, October.

Halsey, A H, Heath, A F and Ridge, J M (1972). 'The Political Arithmetic of Public Schools' in Walford G (Ed) *British Public Schools: Policy and Practice*, Falmer Press, Lewes.

Hamblin, A (1974). *Evaluation and Control of Training*. McGraw Hill, London.

Handy, C (1987). *The Handy Report: The Making of Modern Managers: A Report on Management Education, Training and Development in the USA, West Germany, France, Japan and the UK*. National Economic Development Office, London.

Handy, C (1989). *The Age of Unreason*, Business Books, London.

Hesseling, P (1966). *Strategy of Evaluation Research in the Field of Supervisory and Management Training*, van Goram and Company, Assen.

Hewstone, M (1988). *Attribution Theory*, Blackwell, Oxford.

Hill, S (1991a). 'How Do You Manage a Flexible Firm? The Total Quality Model,' *Work, Employment and Society*, Vol. 5, No. 3.

Hill, S (1991b). 'Why Quality Circles failed but Total Quality might succeed', *British Journal of Industrial Relations*, Vol. XXIX No. 4 (December).

Ishikawa, K (1985). *What is Total Quality Control? The Japanese Way*, Prentice Hall, Englewood Cliffs, New Jersey.

Jowell, R, Witherspoon, S and Brook, L (Eds) (1987). *British Social Attitudes: the Fifth Report*, Gower, Aldershot.

Juran, J, Gryna, F and Bingham, R (Eds) (1974). *Quality Control Handbook* (3rd Ed), McGraw Hill, New York.

Kaelble, H (1985). *Social Mobility in the 19th and 20th Centuries: Europe and America in Comparative Perspective*, Berg, Leamington Spa.

Keeble, S P (1984). *University Education and Business Management from the 1890s to the 1950s: A Reluctant Relationship*, Unpublished PhD Thesis, University of London.

Keep, E (1989). 'Corporate Training Strategies: The Vital Component?', In Storey, J (Ed). *New Perspectives on Human Resource Management*, Routledge, London.

Kotter, J (1982). *The General Managers*, The Free Press, New York.

Lazonick, W (1986). 'Strategy Structure and Management Development in the United States and Britain' in Kobayishi, K and Morikawa, H (Eds) *Development of Managerial Enterprise: proceedings of the International Conference on Business History*, University of Tokyo Press, Tokyo.

Lea, H D (1981). *Relationship of Levinson's Concepts of Dream and Mentor to the Psychological Consistency and Congruence of Work Histories*, Dissertation, University of Maryland, Maryland.

Levinson, D J, Darrow, D N, Klein, E B, Levinson, M H and McKee, B (1978). *The Seasons of a Man's Life*, Ballantine Books, New York.

Leadbeater, C and Lloyd, J (1987). *In Search of Work*, Penguin Books, London.

Lewis, J (1954). *Partnership for All*, London.

Libassi, F P (1988). 'Integrating the Elder in the Labor Force: Consequences and Experience for Insurance', *The Geneva Papers on Risk and Insurance*, Vol. 13, No. 49.

Lillrank, P and Kano, N (1989). *Continuous Improvement: Quality Control Circles in Japanese Industry*, Center for Japanese Studies, The University of Michigan, Ann Arbor, Minneapolis.

Lundvall, D (1974). 'Quality Costs,' in Juran, J, Gryna, F and Bingham, R (Eds). *Quality Control Handbook* (3rd Ed), McGraw Hill, New York.

McKendrick, N and Outhwaite, R B (Eds) (1986). *Businessmen and Public Policy: Essays in Honour of D C Coleman*, Cambridge University Press, Cambridge.

Mangham, I and Silver, M (1986). *Management Training: Context and Process*, Economic and Social Research Council, London.

Mannari, H (1974). *The Japanese Business Leaders*, University of Tokyo Press, Tokyo.

Margerison, C (1980). 'How Chief Executives Succeed', *Journal of European Industrial Training*, Vol. 4, No. 5.

Margerison, C and Kakabadse, A (1985). 'What Management Development Means for American CEOs', *Journal of Management Development*, Vol. 4, No. 5.

Meade, J E (1989). *Agathotopia: The Economics of Partnership*, Aberdeen University Press, Aberdeen.

Mumford, A (1988). 'Developing Managers for the Board', *Journal of Management Development*, Vol. 7, No. 1.

Mumford, A (1989). *Management Development: Strategies for Action*, Institute of Personnel Management, London.

OECD (1988). *Ageing Populations: the Social Policy Implications*, Paris.

Oakland, J S (1989). *Total Quality Management*, Heinemann, Oxford.

National Alliance of Business (1986). *Employment Policies: Looking to the Year 2000*.

PA Consulting Group (1986). *Management Development and Mentoring: an International Study*, London.

Parkinson, C N (1986). *Parkinson's Law*, Penguin Books, London.

Personick, V (1985). 'A Second Look at Industry Output and Employment Trends through 1995', *Monthly Labor Review*.

Peters, T (1989). *Thriving on Chaos: Handbook for a Management Revolution*, Pan, London.

Phillips-Jones L (1982). *Mentors and Proteges*, Arbor House, New York.

Political and Economic Planning (1956). *Graduate Employment: A Sample Survey*, Allen & Unwin, London.

Price Waterhouse (1988-89). *Managing Information Technology*, International Survey. London.

Price Waterhouse (1989-90). *Managing Information Technology*, International Survey. London.

Rubinstein, W D (1986). 'Education and the Social Origins of British Elites 1880-1970', *Past and Present* No. 112.

Rubinstein, W D (1988). 'Social Class, Social Attitudes and British Business Life', *Oxford Review of Economic Policy*, Vol 4, Spring.

Saari, L, Johnson, T, McLaughlin, S and Zimmerle, D (1988). 'A Survey of Management Training and Education Practices in US Companies', *Personnel Psychology*.

Sanderson, M (1972). *The Universities and British Industry 1985-1979*, Routledge & Kegan Paul, London.

Schein, E (1985). *Organizational Culture and Leadership*, Jossey Bass, San Fransisco, USA.

Schmahl, W (1989). 'Labour Force Participation and Social Insurance Systems' in Johnson, P, Conrad, C and Thomson, D (Eds) *Workers versus Pensioners: Intergenerational Justice in an Ageing World*. Manchester University Press, Manchester.

Silverton, G T and Lukasiewicz, J (1985). 'Occupational Employment Projections 1984-95 Outlook', *Monthly Labor Review*.

Stanworth, P and Giddens, A (1974). *Elites and Power in British Society*, Cambridge University Press, Cambridge.

Storey, J (Ed) (1989). *New Perspectives on Human Resource Management*, Routledge, London.

Sveilby, K E and Lloyd, T (1987). *Managing Knowhow*, Bloomsbury, London.

Syrett, M (1990). *Financial Times,* 24 July.

Tate, P (1988). 'Risk! The Third Factor', *Datamation,* April 15.

Taylor, S (1989). *Employee Ownership and Economic Performance: A Comparative Study of the John Lewis Partnership with its Main Retailing Competitors*, Unpublished PhD Thesis, London School of Economics.

Thomas H (Ed) (1959). *The Establishment*, Anthony Blond, London.

Tichy, N, Fombrun, C and Devanna, M (1982). 'Strategic Human Resource Management', *Sloan Management Review*, Vol. 23, No. 2.

United States General Accounting Office (1979). *Analysis of Nine US Federal Projects*, FGMSD-80-4.

Universities Grants Commission (1968-80). *Detail of 1st Destinations of University Graduates.*

Universities Grants Commission: *On Admissions, Annual Reports, 1968-69-1987-88, Statistical Supplements.*

Walford, G (Ed) (1972). *British Public Schools: Policy and Practice*, Falmer Press, Lewes.

Wallace Bell, D and Hanson, C (1987). *Profit-Sharing and Profitability*, Kogan Page, London

Warren, W L and Abegglen, J C (1955). *Occupational Mobility in American Business and Industry*, Minneapolis.

Weiner, B, Frieze, I, Kukla, A, Reed, L, Rest, S and Rosenbaum, R (1971). *Perceiving the Causes of Success and Failure*, General Learning Press, Morristown, New Jersey.

Wiener, M J (1981). *English Culture and the Decline of the Industrial Spirit 1850-1980*, Cambridge University Press, Cambridge.

Weitzman, M (1984). *The Share Economy: Conquering Stagflation*, Harvard University Press, Cambridge, Massachussetts.

Weizenbaum, J (1976). *Computer Power and Reason*, Freeman, New York.

Wilkins, A L (1989). *Developing Corporate Character*, San Fransico, California.

Young, H (1989). *One of Us: A Biography of Margaret Thatcher*, Macmillan, London.

Index

For Product Safety Concerns and Information please contact our EU
representative GPSR@taylorandfrancis.com Taylor & Francis Verlag GmbH,
Kaufingerstraße 24, 80331 München, Germany

Printed and bound by CPI Group (UK) Ltd, Croydon, CR0 4YY
08/05/2025
01864391-0005